THE MADRIGAL

D0005936

Music

Editor

SIR JACK WESTRUP
MA, B.MUS, FRCO, HON.D.MUS
formerly Heather Professor of Music
in the University of Oxford

THE MADRIGAL

Jerome Roche
Lecturer in Music
in the University of Durham

HUTCHINSON UNIVERSITY LIBRARY
LONDON

HUTCHINSON & CO (*Publishers*) LTD
3 Fitzroy Square, London W1

London Melbourne Sydney Auckland
Wellington Johannesburg Cape Town
and agencies throughout the world

First published 1972

*This book has been set in Bembo type, printed in Great Britain
on smooth wove paper by Anchor Press, and
bound by Wm. Brendon, both of Tiptree, Essex*

ISBN 0 09 113260 6 (cased)
0 09 113261 4 (paper)

CONTENTS

And what if she had seen those glories fade,
   Those titles vanish, and that strength decay,—
Yet shall some tribute of regret be paid

When her long life hath reach'd its final day:
Men are we, and must grieve when even the shade
Of that which once was great is pass'd away.

WORDSWORTH
from On the extinction of the Venetian Republic

PREFACE

The history of the madrigal is largely the history of the Italian madrigal, a fascinating, ever-changing yet homogeneous development lasting from 1530 until well into the seventeenth century, to which the transalpine madrigal of England and of northern Europe formed two satellites. To some English readers, familiar with English madrigals to the exclusion of all others, such a view may seem a little disorientating at first. To others, more cosmopolitan in their interests, it may be necessary to defend the exclusion of any consideration of French, German or Spanish secular music, despite arguable parallels between these and the madrigal. The madrigal is essentially an Italianate art-form, and only the Italianate manifestations and principal off-shoots have been regarded as coming within the scope of this book.

Inevitably, any writer on this subject labours in the shadow cast by Einstein's monumental study *The Italian Madrigal* of 1949 and, in the case of the English development, by Kerman's more recent *The Elizabethan Madrigal*. The reader is advised to refer to these excellent works for a fuller consideration of the literary background to the madrigal than has been attempted here. Without playing down the evident importance of poetic aspects, the present study dwells mainly on the musical developments in madrigal composition and is addressed to musicians and music-lovers who may not be as well versed in poetry as readers of Einstein's study need to be. It has drawn on the increasing number of editions that have been published since Einstein's day, even though his third volume (consisting of transcriptions) still provides a valuable source for the less well-charted areas of madrigal composition.

So that the book may be used as a work of reference as well as a guide, and in order to avoid continual footnoting of madrigal titles, an alphabetical index of all the madrigals discussed, and their sources in modern editions, is appended, and each madrigal is also listed under its composer in the general index.

Durham University   JEROME ROCHE

I

FROTTOLA AND MADRIGAL—

DISTINCTIONS AND BEGINNINGS

The best kind of [light music] is termed Madrigal, a word for the etymology of which I can give no reason; yet use showeth that it is a kind of music made upon songs and sonnets such as Petrarch and many poets of our time have excelled in . . . It is, next unto the Motet, the most artificial and, to men of understanding, most delightful.[1]*

Thus the English theorist and composer Thomas Morley describes the madrigal in his *Plaine and Easie Introduction*. It is a description which, though written for English readers in the last years of the sixteenth century, does justice to the whole concept of the Italian madrigal. Today we can be no more certain about the etymology of the word 'madrigal' than Morley was: a commonly accepted view is that it derives from 'mandra'—flock, hence a 'pastoral song'; this would account possibly for the connections between the madrigal and pastoral poetry that are prominent at times in its development.

But even before the sixteenth century the word madrigal had been current in Italy. It also refers to a flourishing form of fourteenth-century secular music set to poems with a distinct rhyme scheme, having stanzas of eight or eleven lines. From a literary viewpoint, the Italian Renaissance was under way in the fourteenth century, and such forms as the madrigal reflected the desire to set new vernacular poetry to music. This period was followed by a large gap during the succeeding century when poetic standards lapsed and literary-musical activity was sporadic, so that when, by the early sixteenth century,

* Superior figures refer to end-of-chapter notes.

there was a movement to revive ancient poetic values, composers adopted entirely new musical techniques even if the poetry itself was freely related to earlier types.

Of the fourteenth-century poets whose work provided texts for the new madrigals, the most important was Petrarch, whose poetry seemed, as Einstein suggests, predestined for this purpose. It deals with unconsummated love, the ideal but unattainable woman, with a feeling of unreality and convention in its formal polish. It was Petrarch's poetry that the new literary movement led by Cardinal Pietro Bembo was concerned to restore, not the ancient Tuscan style of Dante, and it is true that the latter's poetry was very rarely set by madrigalists. Other more modern poets included Sannazzaro, author of *Arcadia* and master of the pastoral atmosphere, whose texts appealed to later madrigalists such as Marenzio, and Ariosto, whose famous *Orlando furioso* (1516) provided a quarry for many composers.

As for the musical antecedents of the early Italian madrigal, we have to look to the frottola style prevalent around the turn of the sixteenth century, which also presents a picture of the rather base poetic standards of the time. The frottola was normally a simple chordal piece in four parts, its phrase lengths determined by the poetic lines: different poetic forms had different structures and rhyme schemes which were closely articulated in the musical form, and the poetry was always strophic. This variety of verse forms and types of composition is present in the frottola collections published by Petrucci at Venice between 1504 and 1514. Whether or not the text was underlaid to all the parts, it was closely related only to the top part, which, though having a narrow range and frequent repeated notes, could often be tuneful. The bass line was angular since it provided harmonic support to the tune; the inner parts, added later, acted as infilling and were again angular, crossing each other to avoid consecutives. Whereas the top part was punctuated by rests, the lower ones were continuous, suggesting instrumental accompaniment. In placing a certain emphasis on the top part, this song style was adaptable to other modes of performance, such as voice and lute—arrangements for this combination were common. Unlike the most advanced sacred polyphony of the time, the frottola contained neither imitation, nor learned devices, and as a result of its harmonic bass line and perfect cadences it was often imbued with a feeling of modern tonality rather than modality.

Before considering the years of transition from frottola to madrigal, let us by way of antithesis look at the salient features of the early madrigal. It strikes a noble and lofty note both in text and music. Upon the simple chordal style is superimposed a motet idiom, so that passages of homophony and imitation alternate. The short text is non-strophic, and the setting therefore continuous, providing the opportunity for a natural correspondence between words and music. Such a correspondence occurs now in all voices, not just the top one. With this equality of voices and more contrapuntal manner, the frottola's strong feeling of tonality fades somewhat.

The transition between these two types, of which the above are somewhat over-simplified descriptions, can be traced equally in the literary and musical spheres, but it was the literary movement which prompted the musical changes. A change in taste towards poetry of higher artistic standard can be witnessed in the sequence of frottola publications of Petrucci: in his Book XI of 1514 there are 25 settings of poems of literary value, of which 20 are by Petrarch. Andrea Antico, publisher and composer, had already begun to stress such values in his *Canzoni Nove* of 1510; after 1514 he took over frottola publication from Petrucci, though pirating from the latter's collections. His *Canzoni, Sonetti, Strambotti et Frottole* of 1517 present a wide variety of poetic types: significantly, *canzoni* and sonnets are placed first in the title, for these represent the serious artistic poems—*canzone* was, in fact, the early name for 'madrigal'. These poems move away from a rigid verse-structure to an irregular one of seven- and eleven-syllable lines in alternation. There is no evidence to support Einstein's idea that the frottolists found difficulty in setting irregular verse lengths and catching the mood of the poem, for the two most distinguished of these, Bartolomeo Tromboncino and Marco Cara, were capable of a considerable degree of expression—indeed Castiglione singles Cara out for praise in his *Il Cortegiano* (*The Courtier*) on account of the 'mourning sweetness' of some of his music. In other words, the madrigal ethos did not arrive from outside Italy with the Franco-Flemings who came south, for it was already being hinted at in the work of the best frottolists. And, of course, Cardinal Bembo's campaign for better poetry—not a campaign for the Latin of high literary discourse but for the Italian vernacular ennobled in the early Renaissance of the fourteenth century—was an impulse towards the madrigal style that came from within Italy itself.[2] The use of the word 'madrigal' reflects the same spirit of resurrection of the Italian past, though the

strict formal pattern of the fourteenth-century madrigal was abandoned
in favour of the single strophe.

In the musical sphere, movements towards the madrigal style were
present in the more elaborate types of frottola with runs in the middle

Example 1

S. Festa, 'O passi sparsi'

[Ah! Stay and see how unhappy I am]

Example 2
Anon, 'Tanto mi trovo'
[Alas, I find my heart so badly wounded]

parts and a measure of vocal independence, composed by Tromboncino and Cara. The music of Antico's publication of 1517, already mentioned, has this independence too, and although there is no imitation it is by no means all homophonic. Another important figure is Michele Pesenti, whose musical style also contains actual imitation; while some of his texts are without merit, he shows a more literary turn of mind in setting odes by Horace.[3]

The transitional decade was that between 1520 and 1530, the date of the first publication bearing the word 'madrigal' on the title-page. During these years Sebastiano Festa, the brother of the better-known

Costanzo Festa, proved to be the link between the frottolists and the early madrigalists. His *O passi sparsi*, printed in a collection of 1526 which represented the changing taste of the day, is largely chordal and does not allow a perfect matching of words and music in the lower voices; but on the other hand there is an expressive feeling, apparent in the descending scale in the top part at 'O bel viso' and especially (as Rubsamen points out)[4] in the repetitions of the last line, with the exclamation 'Deh!' sung to a prominent long-held chord (see Example 1). His delightful setting of *L'ultimo dì di maggio* is really a *villotta*, one of the light forms that succeeded the frottola, but in its textural variety it has much in common with the early madrigal. Sebastiano Festa, whose music was published in France as well as in Italy, provides a connection between the Paris chanson and the embryonic madrigal, which was to adopt certain traits from French secular music. In fact Italy in the 1520s can be viewed in this way as a melting-pot for a style compounded of many diverse elements, whether French, Franco-Flemish or Italian.

Perhaps the most advanced style of the transitional decade is to be found in the anonymous *Tanto mi trovo*, a long setting of a Petrarchian text in fully contrapuntal style without any repeated section, of which Example 2 shows the opening bars. This certainly shows how some composers had already made strides forward from the simple homophony of the frottola.

1. T. Morley, *A Plaine and Easie Introduction to Practical Music*, Ed. R. A. Harman (London, 1952), p. 294.
2. D. Mace, 'Pietro Bembo and the Literary Origins of the Italian Madrigal', *Musical Quarterly*, lv (1969), p. 65.
3. W. Rubsamen, 'From frottola to madrigal', in *Chanson and Madrigal 1480–1530*, Ed. J. Haar (Cambridge, Mass., 1964), p. 67.
4. ibid., pp. 69–70.

2

THE EARLY ITALIAN MADRIGALISTS

Another excellent example of the transitional style is provided by Costanzo Festa's *Quando ritrova*, which shows that the chordal type of earliest madrigal had made little advance on the frottola. This piece is well known to English singers as 'Down in a flow'ry vale'. It unfolds in short, clipped phrases in which the feminine rhythmic ending so common in the frottola is prominent, though the opening bar has a long-short-short rhythm characteristic of the French chanson and of what was later called the 'narrative' style. Indeed, Reese aptly describes *Quando ritrova* as a French chanson with Italian text,[1] an assertion that can be justified when we remember that the chanson had close connections with the frottola style as a result of exchanges both cultural and military between France and Italy. That it is not as yet far from a popular style is also shown by the rather crude consecutive fifths in the second bar, a usage later to be cultivated in the popular types of piece that succeeded the frottola.

This chapter is largely concerned with the work of three composers— Festa, Verdelot and Arcadelt—of whom Festa was the only native Italian. His date of birth is not known, but it must be after 1480; he came from Turin in the far north but spent much of his life in Rome, being a member of the Papal chapel choir from 1517, though he also had connections at Florence. He died in 1545. Whereas most of his madrigals appeared not in separate publications of his own music but in anthologies, those of Verdelot and Arcadelt also appeared in separate volumes. Venice, which harboured the music-printing trade, saw the flood gates of madrigal output open in the year 1533 with Verdelot's Book I of four-part madrigals, and before the decade was out this man had produced a whole stream of volumes, the contributions being from his colleagues as well as himself. Arcadelt in his turn published four volumes in the single year 1539. The incredible popularity of these madrigals in the context of sixteenth-century musical life is measured by the fact that Verdelot's first two books received fourteen printings between the 1530s and the 1560s, and that Arcadelt's Book I appeared no fewer than 33 times during a period of well over a century—a genuine best-seller and this in an age of disposable music.

What purpose did such a corpus of music serve? The answer is provided by the rapid growth of humanist culture and the needs of the new upper middle class as well as aristocratic court circles. We have seen how the birth of the madrigal depended on a literary movement. What was required was an art form that combined poetry and music and would appeal to the man of culture, not just to the brilliant intellectual. It became an accepted thing to foregather for a session of madrigal singing, not so much in the private home as in the cultural academy, a kind of club whose members met for all manner of intellectual betterment. The madrigal was therefore a convivial chamber music that did not require the presence of an audience. In the context of court life it could, however, play a different part. Some pieces, whose style stands apart from that of the rest, were clearly intended as music for ceremonial occasions, and several examples of Festa's work formed part of the musical accompaniment to a spectacular entertainment staged in honour of the Duke of Florence's marriage in 1539.[2] Although this was a great court occasion, the entertainment was comprehensive in scope and directed towards not only the aristocracy but also other more humble levels of society. The festivities began with ceremonial arrivals to the background of a sonorous motet, followed by a banquet and pageant, in which various accompanying madrigals symbolized the possessions of the Duke; and finally the performance of a comedy whose acts were interspersed with *intermedii* in the form of more madrigals sung and played in costume. But whether madrigals were intended as interlude music in a play or as the delight of private gatherings, they should be seen as part of a *Gesamtkunstwerk*—a total artistic picture—of their period, and as a manifestation of the humanist spirit that related art more and more to everyday life.

The madrigal was born of the contact between northern composers (ignoring Festa for the moment) and Italian poets. Who were these non-Italians? Philippe Verdelot, born in about 1480, came originally from the south of France and could possibly have studied with Obrecht in Ferrara; he is known to have worked in other north Italian cities such as Venice and Florence. More than any other composer he launched the madrigal on its way, and yet no madrigal collections of his appeared after 1540, though he did not die till around 1552. Though his compositions were contemporary, Jacques Arcadelt was a younger man, born probably just after 1500. In Florence before 1539, he spent the 1540s in Rome as a member of the Papal choir, which contained many northerners who had migrated south (Festa, it should be noted, was not only one of the few Italians to write madrigals at this early stage, he was one of the few in this choir). Arcadelt later returned north, being choirmaster to the royal chapel in Paris in 1557. He died about 1572.

As for its musical elements, the early madrigal presents a synthesis of Franco-Flemish polyphonic techniques, as developed to a new degree of assurance in the works of Josquin and his pupils, and the far simpler song-style of the Italian frottola. The standard four-part texture of both these genres was maintained in the early madrigal, and although it was soon superseded by the five-part one, let us for the time being restrict the discussion to this more 'classical' texture. From the outset it is clear that the northerners were attracted by the more lyrical features of the indigenous Italian song-style, for despite the more contrapuntal fabric of their early madrigals the voices had not yet achieved equality; the top part, with its tuneful nature, still asserted its superiority. Its distinction of character could be effected by reserving for it all the cadential suspensions that the composer would ornament in his original or the singer would improvise in performance, or by detaching it from a contrapuntal argument confined to the lower three voices. A more obvious way to make it stand out was to keep it in a fairly high register, well above the alto, which would hardly ever cross it: this is a particular feature of Arcadelt's four-part madrigals, and accounts for their lyrical quality. We should remember, too, that Arcadelt was a writer of French chansons, whose style also had roots in Italian lyricism, and that clarity of part writing was the hallmark of the work of the best *chansonnistes*.

Arcadelt's most famous madrigal, *Il bianco e dolce cigno*, illustrates the song-style at its best: it was very successful at the time and was still in demand many decades later, not only as a madrigal to sing but also

as a model for aspiring composers and writers of Masses based on
madrigals. Its text was to be the model for that of Gibbons's equally
well-known *The Silver Swan*. This is less a contrapuntal creation than
a beautifully harmonized melody, whose accompaniment flowers into
independent writing only at the end. Just as the frottola had been
susceptible of performance by different types of ensemble—four

Example 3
Arcadelt, 'O felici occhi miei'
[Happy (eyes) that are
Dear to my beloved]

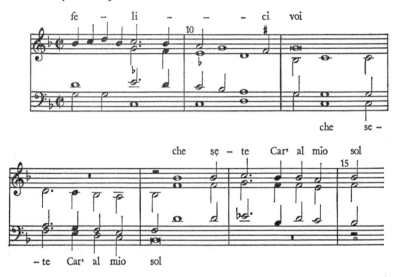

voices; voice and three instruments; voice and lute—so it is here;
whereas the second of these interpretations will accentuate the song-
like feeling, even if the accompaniment is quite contrapuntal, the
purely vocal one will emphasize a homogeneous sonority that later
took on greater importance for the madrigalists. Another of Arcadelt's
pieces, *O felici occhi miei*, will respond to such treatment. The top line,
having the simplicity of a French chanson, seems to call for a vocal
solo, but four voices are needed if the delicate contrasts of colour in
bars 11–15 are to come across (see Example 3). The falling 6/3 chords
over a static bass at the opening also sound stronger in an all-vocal
rendering.

How did the technique of imitation, that most characteristic feature of the mature Franco-Flemish motet, touch upon the early development of the madrigal? Certainly it never became consistently used for the openings of pieces, for it was an abstract musical device appropriate in sacred music for spinning out the exposition of a musical idea set to neutral words. In the madrigal, where poetic considerations loomed as large as musical ones, the opening was often compressed in order

Example 4
Verdelot, 'Madonna il tuo bel viso'
[My lady, your beautiful face]

to project the text more forcefully: if not actually chordal, as many of Verdelot's were, it would bring in two or three voices together or in quick succession without much regard for thematic relationship between the voices. For a fine example of an imitative motet-like opening, here is Verdelot's *Madonna il tuo bel viso* (Example 4), which shows a typical pair treatment and a fine balance of opposing lines at the end. Normally, however, imitation was less a structural principle than a means to variety within a madrigal. Whereas in the motet a chordal passage provided a contrasted interlude in a basically imitative style, in the madrigal the music was still to some extent conceived vertically and the imitation provided the interlude. This

is especially true of Festa's two madrigals written for the Duke of
Florence's wedding entertainment in 1539. *Più che mai vaga* has hardly
any imitation, *Come lieta si mostra* has rather more, but since they had
to be sung by heart as part of a pageant (presenting to the Duke symbols
of his possessions), they were written in a simple style.

Pair treatment was mentioned above: this was another legacy of
the Josquin style, taken up by the French chanson writers and the early
madrigalists in their quest for delicate contrasts of colour. At its
simplest it could paint the words delightfully, as in Example 5, from
Verdelot's *Ogn'hor per voi sospiro*, by contrasting pairs of voices.
Another common device was that of stating a musical idea on two

Example 5
Verdelot, 'Ogn'hor per voi sospiro'
[Being silent, or loving with an amorous fire]

voices and then adding the other two—straightforward double counterpoint in fact—and if the two-part phrase was several bars long this
would bring variety by thinning the texture often in response to the
demands of the text.

Sometimes the treatment of part-writing and dissonance could be
primitive. Near the beginning of the Verdelot piece just mentioned
there occurs a rough double suspension with the inner parts moving
in stark fourths, which can hardly be to paint the words, and in
Festa's *Dur'è'l partito* we find a linear approach at cadences resulting
in some curious false relations, one of which is simultaneously sounded.
On the other hand the madrigal's great reliance upon well-balanced
sonority could lead to a warmer use of dissonance. The heat is indeed
turned on at the end of this same piece, where the poet pleads for his
chilled feelings to be thawed with 'il vostro caldo' and Festa warms to
this theme with a succession of suspensions (Example 6). This pedal
effect is typical of very many early madrigals, providing a kind of coda

Example 6
C. Festa, 'Dur'è'l partito'
[Your ardour]

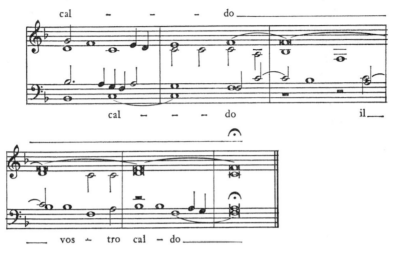

after the final perfect cadence. It is found, also associated with suspensions, at the end of Arcadelt's elegiac *Deh come trista dei*, whose mood is generally intensified by the use of all the sophisticated dissonances of mature Franco-Flemish polyphony. Arcadelt was thoroughly versed in the art of exquisite harmonic colouring in a four-part medium, and his chording has an especial warmth in the fine *Voi ve n'andate*, whether in the double suspensions (bars 50–51: much less stark than in Festa and Verdelot) or in the 'added sixth' type of harmony in the last bars. But despite these variations in approach to harmonic detail, the early madrigalists preserved a strict adherence to the modal system as handled by Josquin. If they chose a major mode, the effect might be more modern, but in a minor one it still had an archaic quality, particularly in the Dorian mode, which could be modified only by the addition of a large number of *musica ficta* accidentals, a practice whose authenticity is at best conjectural. For instance, Festa's *Più che mai vaga*, in the Dorian mode on G with one flat, has no written-in accidentals save a few E♮s that are essential in their contexts, and it was (and is) up to the performers to decide such things as whether to make the final plagal cadence C major–G minor, or C minor–G major, or even a combination of the two.

If the degree of modal archaism was sometimes a matter for doubt, the actual pitch-level of early madrigals was not so, and there appeared a clear distinction between the normal SATB clef combination and lower groupings such as ATTB or TTTB, which afforded new sonorous possibilities. The reason for the quite widespread use of such *voci pari* scorings can be related to the actual cult of Petrarch texts, for there is nothing more appropriate than a low male-voice group, symbolising the aspiring lover, to serenade Petrarch's ideal woman, the Madonna, the passive listener to such plaints. On the other hand we are reminded that nymphs were not after all feminine beings when we discover that Festa's *Più che mai vaga* is scored for TTTB, to be sung by 'Flora', perhaps with her nymphs, as an offering to Duke Cosimo of Florence in his marriage pageant. Otherwise it is hard to account for this scoring, and though it could, of course, have been rendered as a solo with accompaniment, the top part is still a man's. In the normal SATB grouping, too, a new awareness of contrasted sonority is noticeable, especially in Arcadelt. We have already encountered a typical example in Example 3, and it is worth comparing bar 25 and bar 34 of his *Voi ve n'andate* to see the great difference of colour between the brilliant F major chord and the sombre C major; nor is it surprising that the respective words being set are 'volo' (I fly) and 'pianti' (plaints).

Arcadelt is, as Einstein says, the classical master of the four-part texture. His madrigals proceed by an easy flow, fusing the song-like chordal manner of the Italians with the non-studious contrapuntal treatment of the Franco-Flemings to produce a varied alternation of homophony and polyphony throughout a piece, and he always fastidiously articulates the text. His interest in sonority was generally amply served by the four-part texture, whereas for Verdelot five voices offered more possibilities, so that we see the native Italian medium gradually losing prominence in his work. Verdelot seems to have chosen the five-part scoring because it afforded many new contrasts of colour without monotony of texture or too much word repetition. The total range of the voices could be extended (though sometimes five parts within a quite limited range could produce an especially rich effect) and with judicious use of the tutti the declamation of the text could be made more dramatic. There was even the possibility of a genuine dialogue between two lovers, represented by high and low groups respectively, which Reese suggests is present in

Verdelot's *Quant'ahi lasso*, though in fact the colours here are more varied still. If we call the second tenor Q (*quintus*), they succeed each other thus: TQB, SATQ, ATQB, AQB, tutti and so on. Such contrasts depend on a fairly wide range between the outer voices, for where the range is narrower (as in *Dormend'un giorno a Bai*, for ATBBB) Verdelot prefers not to play off varied groupings but rather to wallow, in motet fashion, in the richness of bottom-heavy sound. Another low

Example 7
C. Festa, 'Mentre nel dubbio petto'
[Said the Hebrew mother]

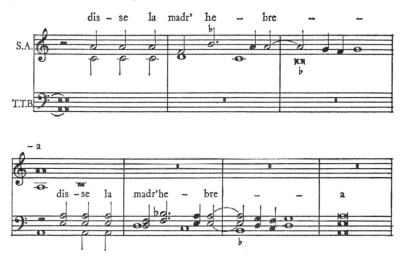

scoring is found in Festa's five-part *Donna ne fu*, whose bass part, written in the contra-bass clef (F_5), is so low that the piece was probably intended for solo voice and viol accompaniment.

In other words, by no means all five-part madrigals were so forward-looking in their use of colour as Verdelot's *Quant'ahi lasso*. Arcadelt's *Gite, rime dolenti*, for instance, shows that he can handle the medium clearly and without opaqueness, but there are no definite textural contrasts, just a constantly altering, but clearly-chorded sonority. Even more archaic in sonority is Festa's *Mentre nel dubbio petto*. The spirit of Josquin is present in the austere modal colouring, and in this lone example of pair alternation (with an extra middle voice between the lower pair to roughen up the suspensions) (Example 7).

The fact that Josquin himself could have conceived the music of Example 7 reminds us that his mature chansons were indeed the earliest prototype of five-part secular music and that it was only logical for madrigalists from the North to adopt a similar style in the first five-part madrigals. In fact contrasted voice groupings had already been tried in Josquin's chansons, growing as they did out of his predilection for pair contrast in the four-part texture. Josquin's contrapuntal mastery had also enabled him to introduce strict canon into chansons, usually between two out of the five voices, without any loss of expressiveness; and although such a learned device failed to find favour with the Italian madrigalists, it can be seen in isolated examples like Arcadelt's *S'infinita bellezza*, where S and TII are in canon throughout. It may be no coincidence that Arcadelt adopts the device in setting not a sentimental love text, but a high-flown, ethical one by Luigi Cassola on the theme of beauty. Other connections with the chanson here are apparent in the frequent dactylic rhythms and repeated notes; the continuously-spun polyphony does not prevent verbal clarity.

This very quality—clarity in declaiming the text—has been mentioned more than once so far; the operative word is 'declaim'. What, we may ask, is the extent to which composers actually expressed the words in this stage of the development of the madrigal? We should remember that the latter grew from a strophic form where one musical section had to serve for several verses of text which might express different emotions. We can see the effect of this in a transitional madrigal by Festa, *Quant'è Madonna mia*, which has repeated musical material: on the word 'morte' (death) we find an expressive falling third B–G (harmonised G–C) in the top part, but on the progression's second appearance the word is now 'vive' (lives). At other times Festa makes a more deliberate effort to paint words. We have already seen the ending of *Dur'è'l partito* in Example 6; the same piece has a naive slowing-down to breves and semibreves at 'andate adagio'. That expression was equally possible in the comparatively rare medium of the three-part madrigal is proved by Arcadelt's graceful *Voi mi poneste in foco*, where the lover's suffering is delineated in subtleties of melodic direction with touches of dissonance. This delicacy of writing removes the piece far from the more popular type of secular music with which the three-part medium was usually associated.

In *Voi ve n'andate* Arcadelt introduces a short chordal passage in triple time to heighten the tension at the words 'ma struggendo mi torno'; the effect here depends on the three semibreves of the triple metre each being faster than the preceding minims of the duple. Such time-signature changes are rare in the madrigal but more common in the chanson. In Verdelot's hands the five-part texture afforded excellent opportunities for dramatic or intimate touches, especially in *Madonna non so dir*. This is an example in which a varied and symmetrically articulated musical layout coexists with the delicate portrayal of both word and mood. The questioning of the poet is admirably captured in the melodic rise and fall and the emphasized middle syllable of the

Example 8
Verdelot, 'Madonna non so dir'
[My lady, I do not (know)]

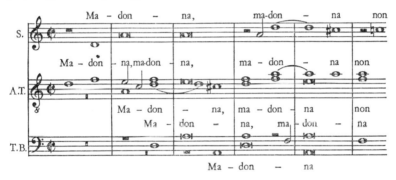

word 'Madonna' (Example 8). Later, his lady's 'yes' and 'no' replies are contemplated with an unusual equanimity on the poet's part, beautifully painted by little answering effects between various two- and three-part groups within the texture. The dramatic gesture comes only when the poet realizes he may be spurned:

> And I, if I cannot be your lover will be my own.

Once again, all five parts reflect this gesture at the words 'and I' ('ed io'): the bass with an octave leap, the tenors with a rhythmically accented motive, the soprano and alto with suspensions.

In discussing the early madrigalists' attitude to rhythm the work of one or two minor composers must be considered. One of these is Jan Gero, another northerner (not to be confused with Maistre Jhan), who was *maestro* at Orvieto cathedral near Rome, and also had con-

nections at Florence, like so many of the early madrigalists. His setting
of *Madonna io vi confesso* is completely dominated by a self-conscious
preoccupation with rhythmic problems, especially syncopation. There
is little melodic interest, lines being scalic or sequential or (in inner
parts) consisting of angular filling in; Gero has none of Arcadelt's feel
for texture or polyphony. Sometimes the syncopation in one voice
is spun out against block motion in the other parts to produce a

Example 9
Gero, 'Madonna io vi confesso'
[But I do not yet wish you to think]

predictable chain of suspensions that has nothing to do with word
expression. Sometimes it has more rhythmic life, though the clumsiness
of the cadence will be noted (Example 9). More delicate, too, is the
grouping of duple-time beats into threes across the (modern) bar-line,
found at chordal moments in this and other early madrigals and often
suggested by the words.

It may have been noticed that Example 9 was in the modern 4/4 (**C**)
time as opposed to the customary minim beats (**₵**) of most of the
earliest madrigals. In fact much of the lighter secular music (*villanelle*
etc.) was normally written in 4/4 with crotchet beats, which were of
course much faster (though not necessarily twice as fast in a strict
proportional rhythm) than the minims of (**₵**). Madrigals written in

4/4 were assigned the description *a note nere* for the very good reason that their crotchets were black notes; and since a crotchet was known as a *chroma* such pieces were called 'chromatic' in the visual, notational sense as distinct from the later, pitch sense. More interesting were the ones in which there was a mixture of slow minim and faster crotchet movement, harnessed to match the rise and fall of tension in the verse. This idea first appears in the work of Francesco Corteccia (1504–71), another native Italian working in Florence: it can be seen in the 4/4 pieces in the *intermedii* performed at Cosimo I's wedding in 1539, and it characterizes even more strongly the madrigal *Se per honesti preghi*, published in a collection of *note nere* pieces in 1543. The text is beautifully articulated by this means: notice how the words 'change to joy' are marked by a return to quick crotchets in Example 10, followed by jerky cross-rhythms that seem to paint the poet's troubled heart. Here, almost by accident, the madrigalists had hit upon a notational nicety that could enhance the faithful declamation of the text. One could go as far as to say that this represented the first attempt at variation of tempo in completely non-sectional music.

Non-sectional, that is, in that few early madrigals were broken up by pauses followed by fresh starts. This is not to say that composers were not concerned to match the musical structure to the poetic form and introduce repeated material or even recapitulation where appropriate. The most common technique was to repeat both the text and the music of the last line of a madrigal, emphasizing its function as the poetic punch-line. Sometimes a brief coda ending with a plagal cadence would be tacked on to add an air of finality, as in this finely-wrought close to Arcadelt's *O felici occhi miei* (Example 11). We can detect a moment of syllabic *note nere* here, which highlights the effect of deceleration in the coda, and also the odd resolution of the dissonant seventh in the tenor. More large-scale musical designs affecting the whole madrigal would often be suggested by the text. In Arcadelt's *Gite, rime dolenti* several of the lines begin with the word 'dove', which he clothes with the same musical motive in such a way that the overall layout becomes ABCB'B—rather like the responsory form in sacred music, and preserving clarity of argument in the rich five-part texture. A genuine textual refrain at the end of each madrigal verse obviously encourages such designs. One occasionally encounters a ternary ABA shape in early madrigals, too. Verdelot has one in *Madonna qual certezza*, where the opening three lines return at the end in the poem,

Example 10

Corteccia, 'Se per honesti preghi'
[Of beauty the least pity
And change to joy my doubtful state
When I was ungrateful for not being ungrateful]

and also in *Madonna il tuo bel viso* where the rhyme scheme is recapitulated at the end though not the words (the music is that of Example 4). In the latter instance he makes a textural contrast for the middle section with more two- and three-part strains to contrast with the more earnest imitative four-part style of the outer ones. One could certainly say, then, that the move away from strophic verse-forms inspired new subtleties of design in the hands of the early madrigalists.

   Of interest by way of conclusion to this consideration of the early madrigal is the work of another peripheral native Italian, Alfonso della Viola, who was connected with the Ferrara court. He was to some extent involved with music for dramatic presentations at the court,

Example 11
Arcadelt, 'O felici occhi miei'
[I chase shadows in my yearning]

but his madrigals, though published at the same time as those of
Verdelot and Arcadelt, can show anticipations of the rich, five-part
textures of Willaert and Rore. This is especially noticeable in the
impassioned setting of *Ingiustissimo amor*, from an anthology published
in 1542. This lacks the clear structural coherence of Arcadelt's *Gite*,
rime dolenti, published in the same collection and sharing the rich
scoring; more attention is paid to varying the pace in each voice and
thus capturing the mood of the text.

Viewing the early madrigal as a whole, however, the prime achievement consists in the perfecting of a clean four-part polyphonic texture,
particularly by Arcadelt, which arose out of the opposed styles of
Franco-Flemish motet and Italian strophic frottola. As yet the five-

part texture was an intriguing new possibility, often handled imagina-
tively by Verdelot, but still not as widespread as it had already become
in sacred music. One thing was certainly not in doubt: the immense
social popularity of the madrigal was a reality among the more cultured echelons of society, a fact attested by the spate of publications
in the 1530s and '40s.

1. G. Reese, *Music in the Renaissance* (London, 1954), p. 320.
2. An account of this entertainment, together with the music performed at it,
   can be found in *A Renaissance Entertainment*, Ed. A. C. Minor and B. Mitchell
   (Missouri, 1968).

3

SERIOUSNESS AND MASTERY

The continuous flow of madrigal collections showed no sign of easing off during the twenty years from 1545, with which we are concerned in this chapter, although the conditions of flood which characterized the 1530s were never again to be matched. This is an interesting fact, for as the above title suggests, the madrigal was inexorably changing its nature—far more quickly than sacred music or even other secular forms outside Italy—at the hands of the two most influential figures of the two decades, Adrian Willaert and Cipriano de Rore. Their work enjoyed a wide dissemination through the flourishing market for madrigal anthologies as well as collections of their own pieces. Certainly Willaert seems to have published little in his own right compared with what we might expect from such a revered doyen of a host of madrigalists.

Although we cannot yet talk of a second generation of madrigal composers, we have emerged by the later 1540s into what Einstein calls the era of the 'post-classic' madrigal. What, then, constitutes the classical madrigal? If it is the four-part output of Verdelot and Arcadelt whose style we have just been exploring, then do we bring the antithesis 'romantic' into discussion at some later stage, or is the word 'classical' used to denote a basic, symmetrical and balanced, perfectly formed style, like that of the eighteenth-century symphony? These are both questionable lines of thought, for on the one hand such concepts are difficult to apply to music of periods other than those with which we usually associate them (and even then they are thought by some to be an unhappy compromise) and on the other, those qualities just mentioned (symmetry, etc.) apply as much to a good deal of

Marenzio's work in the 1580s as to Arcadelt's in the 1530s, and yet many changes came about in those fifty years. The madrigal, as Einstein saw, is a rather freakish development in musical history: it is therefore hard to apply normal critical catch-phrases to it.

The fundamental problem still facing the madrigalists and resolved in Willaert's serious madrigals was how to reconcile Petrarchan poetry with a polyphonic musical medium in an artistic fusion that might appeal to poet and musician alike. We return to Mace's ideas on Cardinal Bembo and his circle, and in particular to his assertion that poetry had a meaning not only intellectual—as any verbal communication—but also affective, through the sounds and rhythms of the words.[1] To put these effects across a polyphonic medium was essential, for the largely homophonic frottola style imposed too much of a rhythmic strait-jacket upon verse. Since Willaert was close to Bembo's followers in Venice, it is no surprise that he took these ideas about a 'sound-unity' of music and words further than Festa and Verdelot. We are not dealing here with overt word-painting or descriptive musical setting but rather with the declamation of words through a harmony that is the sum total (and more) of individual vocal lines. It is this that Zarlino describes in his *Istituzioni armoniche* of 1558 (paraphrased by Morley later). The sound of the words, Mace points out, provides the link between their rational meaning and how they can be expressed in music: the language gives the clue. This can be compared with the eighteenth-century idea that sound meant nothing of itself and that an act of intelligence was necessary to interpret its significance. Such considerations emphasize the fact that the madrigal in its most serious form was the preserve of an intellectual élite, justifiable in terms of the loftiest artistic concepts; from the earthy level of the frottola it had risen in two decades to the rarefied realms of the academic atmosphere.

Willaert (c. 1480–1562) was probably born in Bruges and studied law and music at the University of Paris. Of the northerners of his generation who came to Italy he lived longest and exerted the greatest influence, numbering among his pupils most of the madrigalists mentioned in this chapter and many others. He arrived in the early 1520s, working in Ferrara at the Este court, which fostered so many influential composers from Obrecht to Gesualdo, and in Milan under Cardinal Ippolito d'Este, before his celebrated appointment as *maestro* at St Mark's, Venice, in 1527, where he remained for the remaining thirty-five years of his life, despite occasional visits to his native Flanders. His four-part madrigals belong for the most part to the earliest decade of madrigal publication, appearing in the collections of Verdelot and others, though in spirit they do not belong entirely to this world. One piece, *Amor mi fa morire*, already looks forward to the style of his maturity: its texture is mostly four-part, without pair alternation or contrast, without clear imitation or homophony (save at the significant words 'grave lamento'), and with the modality and the sense of recapitulation—of both words and music—considerably obscured. If this sounds a negative description, the piece itself is none the less the work of a master; it simply lacks the easily defined musical attributes of some of Verdelot or Arcadelt's four-part madrigals. Willaert's better-known essays in this medium are in fact of the *villanella* type, to be considered in Chapter 6.

Willaert was quick to seize the opportunities offered by richer groupings of voices, particularly the five-part texture with which Verdelot had been experimenting, and which would have already been familiar to him from the Franco-Flemish sacred polyphony of his native north. His five-part madrigals demonstrate a new approach to form in articulating the text. Even in the four-part one mentioned above the return of the opening words prompts a free musical reprise —a fairly predictable procedure—whereas a Verdelot piece may have a musical reprise without a verbal one, as in *Madonna qual certezza*. In setting sonnets Willaert now divided the 8-line verse off from the 6-line verse so that the *ottava* and *sestet* (to give them their correct names) made two distinct musical sections, or *partes*. This could be compared with the practice of dividing long motets into *partes* when the sacred text was too cumbersome for a single musical paragraph; but whereas motet texts, often consisting of somewhat ungracious prose, did not themselves suggest subdivision, the sonnet could acquire greater meaning through this treatment. A new slant of poetic imagery in the *sestet* could be more easily underscored after a fresh start in the music, as in *Mentre che'l cor*. After the fairly continuous movement of the *ottava*, the *sestet* opens with the words 'quel foco e morto' in a slow, long-breathed setting, all the more effective after a pause.

What distinguishes Willaert most from Verdelot in the five-part madrigals is his rich scoring. Voices seldom have long rests, and Willaert is much more interested in articulating the text through a

combination of lush harmony and often quite angular part-writing
than by varying the texture in Verdelot's manner. It is in some respects
like a comparison between Josquin and Gombert in sacred music;
but Willaert needed no sacred model other than himself, for his
church music shows the same qualities to the same extent. For him
the vertical aspect, the concern for euphonious harmony, was more
important than historians sometimes allow, and it can be shown
that he was perhaps more conscious of the triad than any polyphonist,
even Palestrina. Such a concern sprang from his activities as a madrigalist, trying to match the beauties of Petrarchan poetry in music.
When he is setting a dialogue, he introduces the device of 'choral
response' into a madrigal, but not in the manner of Verdelot (*Madonna
non so dir*) or of Josquin's five-part chansons; the variation is more
subtle, between voices 1234 and 2345, with just a slight change of
weight and colour. In madrigals for larger ensembles the dialogue idea
is taken further, with greater contrasts of timbre, and in an eight-part
piece like *Quando nascesti, amor*, the double-choir technique is employed
implying a spatial separation of the groups derived from church
music. For it must be remembered that Willaert fostered the growth
of the antiphonal psalm for separated choirs—*cori spezzati*—that
became common in north Italian churches early in the sixteenth
century. With regard, then, to matters like colour and contrast, it is
impossible to separate Willaert the madrigalist from Willaert the
church composer and *maestro* at St Mark's, and it is no coincidence
that his great publication *Musica Nova* (1559), which appropriately
contained the fruit of these new lines of thought, consisted of a mixture
of madrigals and motets—a most unusual idea at the time.

It hardly needs repeating that the most important advances, represented in this publication especially, were in the technique of declaiming words. Phrases from Einstein's assessment spring constantly to
mind: painstaking diction, an inner rhetoric as opposed to the crude
imitation of nature, the art of the restrained *espressivo*. Again, *Mentre
che'l cor* provides an example, with its little rashes of melisma on the
word 'cantando'—the only moment the voices take wing in this way—
or the forward-progressing circle of fifths for 'avanzando' (in the
six-line section). Here is the very mild dissonance at the end, approached
in the soprano by an expressive rising sixth (Example 12). Willaert's
progress does not lead towards the detailed word-painting of some
later madrigalists but rather towards the experiments with choral

Example 12
Willaert, 'Mentre che'l cor'
[And weep sweet tears]

declamation made by Wert and Monteverdi. None the less it belongs to the very beginnings of the 'second practice' later explained by Monteverdi, for the words are master of the music.

During his years at Venice, Willaert taught not only Rore, to whom we shall return later, but also a group of talented lesser composers, whose madrigals show his traits clearly. They were all Venetians who, whether associated with St Mark's or not, were well placed to get their works published by the Venetian printing presses. Girolamo Parabosco was both poet and madrigalist, writing many of the texts set by later composers. His five-part setting of Petrarch's *Aspro cor* parodies that of his teacher, with the mildest of 6/3 chords on the first word, but his texture is more economical than Willaert's: he has two three-part groups of contrasted colour for the twice-repeated opening line. Baldassare Donato was an organist at St Mark's who lived till

1603 but whose secular output dates from before 1570. We find a
rich, Gombert-like scoring in his six-part *I vidi in terra*: a soprano over
five constantly interweaving lower voices. Here it is worth noting
that Donato inserts a very short rest before the word 'sospirando'
(sighing) for a quick intake of breath that will point the word. There
is the same contrast of animation before and after the pause that divides
the *prima* and *seconda parte* as in the Willaert example mentioned
earlier. Here is Donato's majestic opening of the latter section, with
its gradually increasing momentum, its forward circle-of-fifths
progression from the single note E to a C minor chord. The music is
purely triadic, without suspensions, but this does not mean that it lacks
expressiveness (see Example 13). Donato's dialogue madrigals are

Example 13
Donato, 'I vidi in terra'
[Love, wisdom, courage, mercy and sorrow]

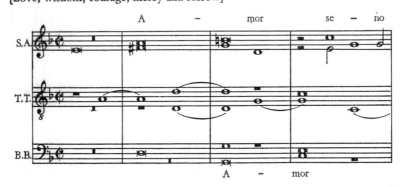

more overtly dramatic and look forward to the madrigal comedy, as can be seen in his 7-part setting of Petrarch's *Che fai alma*, in which each line is given to various freely mixing groups in dialogue (e.g. 1357, 2456; 13457, 1356; 123567 and lastly tutti). Both these Donato madrigals draw upon Willaert's settings, including Example 13 itself.

Willaert's circle included the theorist Gioseffo Zarlino (1517–90), who came to Venice in 1541 to study with him and succeeded Rore as *maestro* at St Mark's in 1565. In his setting of Petrarch's *I'vo piangendo* we again find the thick five-part texture favoured by his teacher, laid out with closely dovetailed imitations. Zarlino shows a reluctance to paint this elegiac text with dissonances, preferring linear means such as angular and syncopated melodic lines. This madrigal was intended to exemplify the increasingly important Aeolian mode, i.e. the normal minor mode of diatonic music, and is written in 'D minor' with a flat. This is in fact transposed Aeolian, but the flat distinguishes it from the flatless Dorian D minor that was still common.

The greatest of Willaert's pupils was Cipriano de Rore (1516–65). He probably came from Antwerp, which was, like Venice, a port and a flourishing musical centre with a music-printing trade, and sang in the choir there till 1534. In around 1547 he was employed at the court of Hercules II in Ferrara, succeeding Vicentino as *maestro* in about 1550. He returned north to Antwerp *via* Munich in 1558 and served in the court of Margaret of Austria at Brussels till 1561. In his last years he was based in Parma, but he occupied the position of *maestro* at St Mark's, Venice, in 1562–3.

If Willaert was the great teacher, the mentor *par excellence* who advocated new ideas in both sacred and secular music, Rore was the one who interpreted these ideas and took them to new heights in the field of madrigal composition, and the one who glimpsed new possibilities. With him the five-part texture, laid out in free polyphony lacking in imitative regularity, now became standardized. But Rore distinguishes himself from his teacher in that his prolific madrigal output is wholly serious in character—the light *villanella* type did not interest him—and that he is more concerned to capture the mood of the texts through musical devices of word-painting: each word must be set as expressively as possible in each vocal line. In this quest for forceful musical expression, he is comparatively indifferent to the form of the poem, the structure of its lines or the consonance of its stanzas.[2]

Not all serious texts are sad, of course; clearly the amount of
emotional underscoring depends on the text, and it can be seen that the
boldest chromatic treatments belong to Rore's most mature period,
when he had been at Ferrara for some years. The earliest pieces,
especially four-part ones, belong to the time of his studies with
Willaert in Venice around 1540 (his own first publication appeared in
1542) and resemble the style of Arcadelt with their melodic poise and

Example 14
Rore, 'Alla dolce ombra'
[To be able to approach the pleasant bowers
 Now life is short]

occasional use of crotchet ('chromatic' in the rhythmic sense) movement. Some of Rore's Book I *à 4*, though not published till 1550,
may well date from this time, particularly a piece like *Alla dolce ombra*.
This is a setting of a *sestina*, a poem in six verses, by Petrarch, with
some archaic polyphonic usages (e.g. the under-third cadence at the
end of verse 3). Rore's excellent sense of timing and contrast is apparent
in this passage from verse 6 (Example 14). Notice also the delicate
ornament in the soprano, and the subtle use of *note nere* for the imitation
on the words 'vita breve'. This contrast of rhythmic animation is
used more dramatically in *Amor, ben mi credevo*, also from Book I
à 4 but more probably written after 1547 in the experimental environ-

ment of Ferrara. Here the music and text of the last two lines is repeated, especially effective in view of two extremely harsh double suspensions on the word 'tormento', and the madrigal literally expires without a final cadence, as the poet bewails his 'living death'. Here is all the forcefulness of expression and darkness of colouring with which the four-part texture could be invested without actual recourse to pitch chromaticism.

This close attention to the meaning of each emotional 'paragraph' in a poem shows bolder manifestations in the last two volumes of five-part madrigals, published in 1557 and (posthumously) in 1566. These are the works in which Rore shows himself to be a harmonic innovator, entirely conversant with the possibilities of the chromatic scale that formed the basis for experiments by Vicentino, his colleague at Ferrara. An excellent example from the fourth book (1557) is *O morte, eterno fin*, whose text is a typical eight-line verse with the rhyme scheme *abababcc*. The very first words introduce a bold extra-modal E♭ (the piece is in transposed Dorian – G minor with one flat) in the tenor, with a wailing effect. That Rore seemed to prefer a varied scoring with plenty of breathing space in each voice part to the rich sonorities of Willaert, can be clearly seen here, for both the second and sixth lines of the verse are lighter in sound, placing emphasis on the fuller scoring of lines 1, 3, 7 and 8. In referring to the rhyme scheme we notice that these are the leading lines of couplets (1 and 3) or the final 'punch-lines' (7–8), and that lines 2 and 6 are following lines of couplets. Line 5, which speaks of 'wretched mortals', is given a quite different kind of emphasis: chromaticism, which serves to remove the music to a B minor chord a major third away from that of the mode (Example 15). There are musical cross-references between the cadences of lines 1 and 3 and the material of lines 2 and 4, showing Rore's keenness for balanced construction.

This is even more apparent in his setting of *Non è lasso martire* from Book V (1566), where the use of musical variation and repetition is subtly harnessed to project the words with greater force. The text helps here, for the opening lines return at the end, prompting a ternary form, but whereas these two lines originally occupied only 12 bars of music, set to what we may call *aa′b*, the return is spread over 26 bars, extended thus: *a′ba′a′b′b″*. It is worth comparing the *b* idea in its first appearance (bar 7) with its final transformation (bar 66) at the end of this much extended—and therefore emotionally heightened—con-

Example 15
Rore, 'O morte, eterno fin'
[Haven of blind and miserable mortals]

cluding paragraph (Example 16). Notice the telling octave drops, the
use of a dark, low register in the third voice, and the brevity of the
last, questioning chord, all marks of a master-plumber of emotional
depths, so to speak. Quite apart from the overall ternary form there
are further repetitions of middle lines to give emphasis to the text, with
the result that there is scarcely a line of the poem that is not sung
twice, with or without variation. Added to this enhancement of the
text by musical structure, there is the clarity afforded by a prepon-
derance of syllabic writing and free homophony, with occasional
clear breaks between musical sentences.

These rests or moments of pause could serve not only as landmarks

Example 16 (a) and (b)
Rore, 'Non è lasso martire'
[The pledge to die for you, lady]

(a)

(b)

during the course of a madrigal, they could also be exploited for dramatic purposes of word-painting. This device is marvellously handled
in one of Rore's best-known madrigals, *Da le belle contrade*. The middle
section of this setting, in which the poet turns from thoughts of bliss
to those of parting, contains two moments of silence (bars 35, 41)
which interrupt a powerful and unexpected succession of harmonies
in a most dramatic way. Not only general pauses are significant;
although the vocal texture may not be interrupted, the rests in each
individual voice at the expostulation 't'en vai, haime!' (thou art going,
alas!) produce a gasping effect that can come through in performance,
and the remarkable falling seventh in the bass only adds to a conviction
that Monteverdi must surely have assimilated the expressive techniques
used in this passage. Nor is this all, for chromaticism has not yet been
mentioned. From the sharpness of an E major chord (bar 36) Rore
moves relentlessly forward (i.e. flatward) through the wrenching A
major–C minor progression interrupted by a rest, to reach the remote
flat chord of D♭ on the word 'joys', and then retraces his steps back to
A major at the end of the section. Here are the words:

> Ah, cruel love,
> Uncertain and brief are thy joys,
> And it even pleases thee,
> That the greatest happiness should end in tears.

This is not melodic chromaticism, but harmonic: in other words,
there are no chromatic alterations (e.g. C♯–C♮) except across the dramatic rest, and it is the sheer range of, if you like, 'key-spectrum'
through which the music passes that was so novel in a period dominated
by the modes and their restrictions. To view the passage another way,
the top part includes every semitone between G and D, including
both G♯ and A♭. It is easy to see that Rore must have been fascinated
by the experiments with an enharmonic scale that were being con-
ducted by others at Ferrara. This harmonic chromaticism completely
dominates the madrigal *Se ben il duol*, couched for the most part in a
homophonic style and showing a scrupulous care for the poetic
quantities that defies modern barring. Chromatic juxtapositions
abound, even in a passage where the texture is reduced (Example 17).
This exquisite composition looks forward to the choral recitative treatment of Wert, and is indeed a far cry from the world of Verdelot and
the 1530s.

The inspiration for Rore's chromaticism must have come in part from the work of Nicola Vicentino (1511–72) who had also studied with Willaert, and served Cardinal Ippolito d'Este in Ferrara. He was a progressive theorist where Zarlino was more conventional, and in his treatise *L'antica musica ridotta alla moderna prattica* (1555) postulated the division of the whole tone into five degrees, thus enabling different types of tone and semitone to be used in differing harmonic contexts. He devised a keyboard instrument, the *arciorgano*, capable of playing these intervals; this might well have been used as a discreet accompaniment to his many chromatic madrigals, to keep the singers in tune with his unfamiliar harmonic effects. One of his finest madrigals is

Example 17
Rore, 'Se ben il duol'
[Which makes me lack strength and courage]

the setting of Ariosto's *O messaggi del cor*. As in other works of his, the musical discourse proceeds from a rather disjointed style with short, halting chordal expostulations in part I to a smoother polyphonic one in part II. In part I, each line of the poem begins with 'O', set in the soprano to a higher note each time, so that the entries start on every semitone between A and E (except B♭). Example 18 includes the most flatward and the most sharpward chords in the madrigal, A♭ and B major; the soprano entries on 'O' have reached D and D♯. It will be seen how each phrase ends with a sighing suspension, quite unresolved by the next harmony, and how the rhythmic tension is vested in the tenor part. Once again, this is the declamatory style that would have inspired Wert.

Another neglected madrigalist is Pietro Taglia of Milan, whose music also belongs to the serious, high-flown atmosphere of Rore and Vicentino. His *Discolorato hai, morte* begins in the unusual modal region of E minor, and contains an episode of quick *note nere* movement

Example 18

Vicentino, 'O messaggi del cor'

[Unjust evil, just lamentings

  O, always intent on thoughts of yearning

  O desire untamed by reason]

concluded by a masterly return to slower note-values in which he displays a gift for timing. His *Valle che de' lamenti* (also *à 5*) is another fascinating anticipation of the style of Wert, this time in its melodic features. It is worth quoting the first 17 bars of the top part in full to show its odd contortions, and its use of the minor seventh as an outline (marked by brackets). The piece is extraordinary also for its true Lydian mode, though the Bs are often flattened, even at bar 11, where one can only conclude that Taglia preferred the augmented fourth in the melody to a false relation with ensuing B♭s in the next chord (Example 19a). The soprano idea of bars 7–9, with its outline seventh, recurs near the end in all the voices, lending consistency to the musical argument by ending the piece in the spirit in which it began (Example 19b).

As has been said, all this music was the preserve of a cultural élite who were more than musicians; poetry and other literary forms and discourse were equally their concern. In Verona, one of the first cultural academies, the *Accademia Filarmonica*, was founded in 1543 to provide for these pursuits. The exclusiveness of the circles for which madrigals were written is attested by the fact that this academy numbered only 13 members, as a painting by its president shows.[3] One of the first composers appointed to direct music there was a Franco-Fleming, Giovanni (Jhan) Nasco, whose duties included writing madrigals on any texts the learned gentlemen members might expect. He was succeeded later by a Veronese, Vincenzo Ruffo (d. 1587), with whose name his is often linked, for some of their published madrigals appeared together in a volume dated 1554, and both held influential church posts in northern Italy at other times in their careers. Nasco's *Madonna quand'io penso* is a gem of five-part writing in the Aeolian mode—less dramatic in its restraint than Rore, but closely matching the music to the sentiments of the text. Thus the imitative point 'when I think of loving' leads to a momentary ray of joy at the dance-like 'my heart is jubilant, free from all trouble' (triple time); but then 'when I think again' returns to the same motive, leading this time to 'how cruel you are' with a heart-rending augmented triad (asterisked) as the new point enters (Example 20). The extra-modal B♮ at bar 33 makes an E minor–G minor false relation that adds to the bitter feeling and recalls one of Josquin's more gloomy chansons, *Parfons regrets*. Nasco's style may indeed be conventional but his harmonic effects are exquisite, as in the double suspension that ends

Example 19 (a)
Taglia, 'Valle che de' lamenti'
[O valley so full of my lamentings
River which often grows with my weeping]

Example 19 (b)
Taglia, 'Valle che de' lamenti'
[Leaving its beautiful remains on earth]

Example 20. It is interesting, too, that he repeats the last line twice, effective for the words 'my grief seems to become greater'.

Practically all the madrigals discussed so far were printed in Venice and represent for the most part composers working in the north of Italy. There was, however, a Roman school of slight significance in the history of the madrigal compared with its standing in the field of sacred music, whose most important master was Giovanni Pierluigi da Palestrina (1525–94). His two collections of secular madrigals—the

Example 20
Nasco, 'Madonna quand'io penso'
[But now when I recall
How cruel you are]

spiritual ones will be mentioned in Chapter 6—date from 1555 and
1586 but by no means constitute his whole madrigal output, for his
considerable influence among publishers and compilers resulted in
quite a number of pieces appearing in anthologies. A comparison
between one of these, the five-verse *canzona Chiare, fresch'e dolci acque*,
with Arcadelt's setting of the same text—both date from the 1550s—
shows Palestrina's writing to be a little humdrum and lacking in

Example 21

Palestrina, 'Voi mi poneste in foco'
[And that the great weeping may not dissolve your heart]

contrasts of texture and style. His manner was quite alien to the
progressive achievements of Willaert and Rore, and he clung to the
four-part texture of Arcadelt even in his Book II of 1586, in which the
only concessions to intense expression consist in a few unconventional
passing notes and double suspensions exemplified in *Alla riva del Tebro*.
This is in no way to diminish the many attractive qualities of his madrigals, qualities that are entirely secular in inspiration and absent in his
church music. In fact too much emphasis has been given to the apparent
similarity between his secular and sacred output, with the result that
the madrigals have been too lightly dismissed. The reality is that, if
we for a moment forget about their anachronistic style *qua* madrigals
and examine them *qua* Palestrina, we can find subtleties of rhythm,
colouring and sequential passages that are never encountered in his

sacred style, and this is partly because he is setting the Italian language instead of Latin. Here is a passage from another *canzona* published in an anthology of 1558, *Voi mi poneste in foco*, which one would hardly guess to be by Palestrina; the treatment of the words 'pianto' and 'core' is especially bold, using the bare fifth and then the augmented triad, with a false relation for good measure (Example 21). Palestrina may well have been out of touch with the activities of Rore and Vicentino, but his madrigals can be pleasing—occasionally even powerful—when viewed side by side with his great corpus of liturgical music.

1. *The Musical Quarterly*, lv (1969), loc. cit.

2. A. Einstein, *The Italian Madrigal* (Princeton, 1949), i, p. 395.

3. ibid., i, p. 455.

4

MUSIC FOR ENTERTAINMENT
AND DELIGHT

Any consideration of the musical history of the 1570s and 1580s presents complex problems, whatever the subject, for it was these decades which witnessed the subtle changes of emphasis that prefigured the Baroque era. Recent research has increasingly shown that musical ideas which became fundamental in the Baroque and in some cases have lasted down to the present century (the concept of balanced tonality and harmonic awareness, for instance) were formulated during these years and that they did not erupt, all of a sudden, in the year 1600 together with the 'invention' of monody and the *basso continuo*. In late Renaissance sacred music the effects of the Council of Trent were now felt in the simple, chordal setting of liturgical texts in order that these should be audible and not concealed within a web of complex counterpoint; musical style was bolder and simpler in colouring than that of masterly polyphonists such as Gombert.

A parallel kind of change became felt, too, in the Italian madrigal. Although one could not speak of polyphonic complexity or lack of regard for the text in the serious mid-century madrigals of Willaert, Rore and their followers, these works boasted a learnedness and loftiness of purpose which, despite its sincerity, appealed perhaps only to the highest echelons of educated society, and tended towards experimentation in realms—chromaticism in particular—that were obscure to all but those versed in theoretical dialogue. What seemed to be called for was a corrective to this over-seriousness—a genre that would not oust it entirely but would be complementary to it, having a lightness of style and content that would appeal widely. Such a type was the purely entertainment madrigal of the 1570s and 1580s with its pastoral leanings, whose boldness and simplicity could well be compared with that of the more up-to-date sacred music: many of the composers were working in both sacred and secular fields anyway. These pastoral leanings became very popular: the texts conjured up an atmosphere of amorous delight where the lovers Phyllis and Corydon played among shepherds and shepherdesses in fields and woods, pierced from time to time by Cupid's arrows, or perhaps languished from the pangs of unrequited love, unable to be consoled by nature. Either way, the music was to reflect every nuance of the words in fanciful, often over-obvious imagery.

The concept of the light *arioso* (i.e. tuneful) madrigal or *madrigaletto* —usually a four-part piece—found some support in the later works of Vincenzo Ruffo, who had been employed at the Veronese *Accademia Filarmonica*, as we have seen. But the pioneer of the type was Andrea Gabrieli (*c.* 1520–86). Unlike Willaert or Rore, he was Italian born, his life being largely based on Venice, where he was a singer and later, from 1564 onwards, one of the organists at St Mark's. A period before this had been spent in the employment of Duke Albrecht V of Bavaria at Munich during the time that Lassus directed music there. This and his other transalpine visits did much to spread the Italian style abroad, and as we shall see in Chapter 7 the mature madrigal had a considerable following in northern Europe. The fact that Gabrieli worked for the Doge in Venice meant that many of his madrigals were for occasions of pomp and ceremony, and for this reason we can detect in some of them the same grandeur that makes his sacred music so impressive. But whereas in the development of sacred music his nephew Giovanni Gabrieli steals the limelight, it is to Andrea that we should turn for the most significant contribution to the madrigal. As Einstein says, he is the pioneer of the fanciful, socially adaptable madrigal: his works had the wide appeal that was needed in a society of both aristocracy and middle class, they were addressed to singers both professional and amateur, and were suitable for occasions both ceremonial and convivial.

One foreign influence in Andrea's lighter madrigals is undoubtedly the French chanson, arrangements of which were currently popular among Venetian organists (of which he was one) in the guise of the *canzona francese*. The tripping, narrative style and characteristic dactylic rhythms of the French manner are evident in his idyllic setting of *Ecco l'aurora*, in which the only concessions to vivid word-painting are a low chord for ATTB on 'night' and a predictable minor inflexion at 'tearful'. This comes from his Book I à 5, published in 1566 at the very beginning of the vogue for the pastoral madrigal. For Andrea Gabrieli colour and sonority—the vertical aspects of music—were all-important. Considerations of line dwindled in significance, imitation points being treated more closely and concisely, so that a madrigal succeeded more by its sequence of exquisite chord colourings and textures. The superb setting of *Laura soave* from the second book à 5 (1570) reveals Andrea's sense of craftsmanship not in its counterpoint—which is almost non-existent—but in his control of harmonic motion and feel for musical shape and variation. Not only do the opening bars, with the affective G minor chord clouding their A minor tonality, reappear at the end of the piece; they are varied upon return by rhythmic compression and then expansion, creating a broad conclusion, and the G minor chord seems to have a more unsettling effect at each repetition. The piece is full of these repetitions, which, whether varied or not, have all the hallmarks of a musical rather than a poetic argument. A case in point is bars 48–58 (Example 22) which presents several approaches to the words 'sentomi morire', each contradicting the harmonies of 'che di dolcezza' by the juxta-posing of unrelated chords. One feels that if Rore were writing this passage he might have ended it not with the confident chordal 'sentomi' but the more dramatic imitative treatment, ending at bar 54 and followed by a telling general pause. But Gabrieli is more concerned with music than drama.

It would be an over-simplification to say that all his madrigals belonged to the light, pastoral type. His *Non vedi o sacr'Apollo*, possibly intended as a chorus for a production of a classical play, has a wide-ranging chromatic spread of keys and an especially intense ending, while the setting of *I'vo piangendo* has the same slow measured tread as the Zarlino setting discussed earlier. In these works Andrea Gabrieli can be seen to look back at the Venetian achievements of his prede-cessors. In other madrigals, as has been suggested, the composer of impressive multichoral sacred music shows through: *Felici d'Adria*, written for the visit of an Austrian nobleman, is a majestic piece in eight parts though not divided into two choirs. This gives a greater amount of freedom to contrast ever-changing voice groupings in a kaleidoscopic approach to colour. For the Venetians by no means always insisted on writing for separated choirs, and were often happy

Example 22
A. Gabrieli, 'Laura soave'
[I feel myself dying of sweetness]

to revel in the sonorous possibilities of an undivided, multiple-voiced ensemble.

The new direction adopted in Andrea's lighter madrigals can be viewed in the context of the Venetian society of the time, a society celebrating with pride the victory over the Turks at Lepanto in 1571, but otherwise having lost some of the commercial and maritime prestige it had had in the middle ages—a decadent and fun-loving community that enjoyed any kind of display. As a reflection of Venetian life, Andrea's madrigals have been compared by Einstein to the paintings of Veronese. This was also the Venice in which his nephew, Giovanni, was brought up under his musical tutelage. Born *c.* 1556, Giovanni spent most of his life in Venice like his uncle, but also had a spell of employment at Munich with Lassus, further cementing the Venetian ties with Austria and South Germany that were to prove so important in the following century. He was second organist at St Mark's, Venice, from 1585 until his death in 1612 but his fame during this time was greater as a teacher, among whose pupils were numbered the Germans, Praetorius and Schütz, to name only the most distinguished.

Andrea must have instilled the art of madrigal-writing into his nephew at an early age, for already in 1575, when Giovanni was still only 18, he had had a madrigal printed in a collection by various 'floridi virtuosi' dedicated to Duke Albrecht of Bavaria. This piece is appropriately a setting of *Quand'io ero giovinetto*—appropriately, that is, until one reads the rest of the text and finds that it is actually the plaint of a lonely old man lamenting his lost youth. Of interest here is the fact that the divided voice in the five-part texture is the soprano, with the result that the upper two parts constantly cross in a kind of dialogue that prefigures the *concertato* style; also the jolly, if conventional, strain of triple time for 'con piacer e gran diletto'. The setting of the final couplet is repeated as usual, with the same rhythmic augmentation of the last phrase that we found in Andrea's *Laura soave*. Even at this early stage Giovanni shows great promise. A more mature piece is the fine *Sacro tempio d'honor*, from an anthology of sonnets published in 1586 (all Giovanni's madrigals appeared in anthologies; they were not gathered together like his church music) and dedicated to Bianca Capello, Grand Duchess of Tuscany. This displays some effective contrasts of register between upper and lower voices and, on a larger scale, a clear distinction between the rhythmically agitated, running music of the central section and the calmer outer sections, the last of which contains repeated music; but notice how the repeat is varied (Example 23) so as to begin in a different key the second time, while still regaining the identical one a few bars later.

Although the five-part texture had been the norm for many years, this is not to say that both the Gabrielis did not write for larger or smaller forces. The Venetian tradition of large-scale pieces like Andrea's *Felici d'Adria* was continued by Giovanni in the massive *Sacri di*

Giove, for an undivided twelve-part ensemble with a characteristic prevalence of lower voices: for clarity one imagines that an orchestra with many trombones would have doubled the singers in the manner normal in church music. It is interesting that this was published in 1587 in a collection entitled 'concerti', containing mostly church music by both Gabrielis. At the other extreme, both could occasionally turn their hands to the dainty art of the three-part madrigal, which came to enjoy a certain limited popularity in this age of the *madrigaletto*. Such pieces had no connection with the coarse *villanella* whose texture they shared, but were often vehicles for a composer's ingenuity in the face of technical limitation, as in Giovanni's delightful *Alma cortese e bella*: for such a restrictive medium the music is well varied, with two upper voices sometimes interweaving over the bass, in the fashion of a Baroque duet, or all three partaking in imitations.

The two Gabrielis were the most renowned of a large circle of Venetian composers which also included Claudio Merulo and Costanzo Porta. Merulo (1533–1604) was Andrea Gabrieli's predecessor as first organist at St Mark's, a post which he held from 1564 till 1584, and otherwise worked in the north Italian cities of Brescia and Parma. His setting of *Quand'io penso al martire*, published in 1566, reveals a lightness of touch that, like Andrea's, was something quite new at that date. Again, this deftness is musical rather than poetic in inspiration, and can be seen in the way the opening idea is presented right-way-up and inverted in clever counterpoint, in the splendid homophonic declamation which ends the *prima parte*, or in the rhythmic cross-accents that follow. There is none of the gloom of Rore or the chromatic intensity of Vicentino, just occasional harsh suspensions or surprising extra-modal chords on the appropriate words, leading to a finely controlled emotional climax (Example 24). Contrast is the keynote: contrast not so much of textures as of sections. Porta (1530–1601) was a Franciscan monk and pupil of Willaert who was *maestro* at various Italian cathedrals. His setting of *Erasi al sole* shares some of the features of Merulo's piece, such as the jaunty rhythms and clear sectional form with dovetailing, but its rather more frivolous text calls for a more pattering word setting, with much syllabic quaver movement which recalls the French chanson. Certainly the airiness of the texture and the economic use of five voices suggest the early style of Marenzio.

Luca Marenzio was the greatest purely madrigal composer in the

Example 23 (a)

G. Gabrieli, 'Sacro tempio d'honor'
[And at the time of death to burn with disdain
 Since he cannot make you (his victim)]

whole history of the Italian madrigal, and the one in whose hands it
reached its culmination as a form with a musical life of its own not
slavishly dependent on its poetry. Born at Coccaglio, near Brescia,
in 1553 or 1554, he was taught by one Giovanni Contino, *maestro*
at the cathedral in this nearby city, but later settled in Rome, where
he made his reputation by publishing a formidable number of madrigal
volumes for between three and six voices. This tremendous success
resulted from a thriving amateur madrigal-singing activity in Rome
which contrasted with the increasingly professional, virtuoso standards
prevailing in some parts of the North. The fact that his madrigal output
was every bit as voluminous as the sacred output of Palestrina, and
that he lived in Rome, was a cause for his being dubbed 'the Palestrina

Example 23 (b)
G. Gabrieli, 'Sacro tempio d'honor'
[And at the time of death to burn with disdain
 Since he cannot make you (his victim)]

of the madrigal', a title which can only confuse the historical positions
of both composers, for the aims of sacred and secular music were quite
different in respect of the words. If such tags are to be applied, a much
more apt one is Arnold's 'the Schubert of the madrigal', an across-the-
centuries comparison which highlights Marenzio's complete fluency
and mastery throughout a prolific output produced largely in the
two decades between 1580 and his death in 1599. Einstein sees Marenzio
as one of the 'virtuoso' composers and as a 'literary' madrigalist, both
of which assertions require some qualification: it is of course his
technique which shows him to be a virtuoso, not the singers for whom
he was writing, while the literary qualities are evidenced by his
tasteful choice of texts rather than in a predominance of literary over
musical appeal. He is the pastoral musician *par excellence*, able to

clothe the ubiquitous tales of nymphs and shepherds, fields and woods, with delightful music. But not all his madrigals paint pictures of such a carefree atmosphere of Arcadian amours, for his later works abandon it for a world of seriousness and mannerist intensity which will be explored later—another justification for comparing him with Schubert.

Example 24
Merulo, 'Quand'io penso al martire'
[O infinite misery]

If there are influences to be found in his early works, the mark of Andrea Gabrieli is most discernible in Marenzio's deftness of touch. *Madonna mia gentil*, from his first book of five-part madrigals (1580), is laid out in a clear ABB form and shows a good grasp of simple answering effects between various voices; the five are hardly ever all used at once. Like Gabrieli, Marenzio wrote a small proportion of four-part madrigals many of which can hardly be called light pieces although the texture was associated with the *madrigaletto*. He published a volume of these in 1585, one of which, *Chi vuol'udir'*, merits some attention before a wider study of the five-part madrigals. The opening words 'He who would hear of my sighs in verse' are set to long-breathed chords with some wide leaps, while 'and of my anguished plaint' is clothed in harsh passing-note clashes leading to a remarkably archaic Phrygian cadence whose dissonant inner fourths match the mood well. Then follows a long paragraph based on two ideas for two lines of

Example 25
Marenzio, 'Chi vuol'udir' '
[For every valley is already full (of my weeping)]

verse, which Marenzio presents separately and then combines in ingenious counterpoints (bars 27–57). The final paragraph (bars 70–93) is also extended, full of syncopations and descending sequences, marvellously effective over the bass of bars 80–84 (Example 25). The way in which the various motives are presented and worked out during each section of the verse is very similar to that adopted by Palestrina in his four-part motets, and we can see that, while acknowledging the normal grace and convention of a four-part madrigal, Marenzio is revelling here in the pure contrapuntal brilliance of a Palestrina and adding some highly individual harmonic and melodic colouring as well.

The majority of Marenzio's madrigals are scored for the established ensemble of five voices, though there is an increasing tendency to use the concerto-like texture of two soprano parts rather than two altos or two tenors. The higher lie of the parts which results from this scoring opens many new opportunities for brilliant colouring that contrasts with the rich hues found in the bottom-heavy five-part writing of earlier madrigalists. Moreover the chording seems to have a more acoustically natural layout when the voices are closest in range at the top of the texture—a feature which emphasises the brightness of jolly, pastoral music. The frequent use of major modes in a guise very similar to modern tonality also contributes to this end.

Like Andrea Gabrieli, Marenzio was called upon to provide ceremonial madrigals, particularly for weddings; *Scendi dal paradiso* (Book IV à 5, 1584) is one such piece, a perfect bond between words and music imploring the descent of Venus from the skies—with a descending motive, naturally. But, having paid due respect to these conventions of word painting, notice the mastery with which Marenzio unfolds the contrapuntal entries (Example 26). Incidentally this idea is strangely prophetic of the subject of the B♭ minor fugue from Book I of the '48'; but whereas Bach's fugue is wholly based upon it, Marenzio's madrigal is a constantly changing patchwork quilt in sound. We should imagine it performed with instrumental doubling for, as listeners' rather than performers' music, it had to impress, and its sound had no doubt to fill a palatial room in some Roman mansion.

The incredible professionalism which is present from Marenzio's very first book of five-part madrigals and which assured his success in Rome in the face of negligible competition, shows through in the famous cantata-like cycle of three madrigals, *Tirsi morir volea*, perhaps the crowning achievement of an impressive opus I. It is not surprising that Nicholas Yonge saw fit to introduce it to the English in his first collection of Italian madrigals, *Musica Transalpina* (1588), under the title *Thirsis to die desired* (the texts were all anonymously 'englished'). The verb 'to die' should of course be understood as a euphemism for the act of love in the context of all pastoral madrigals, among which this one is pre-eminent. For why else would a madrigal text describe a death which its 'victims' should wish to repeat by coming to life again? Viewed in this light, *Tirsi* represents an essay which errs on the side of eroticism, though one can be sure that sixteenth-century madrigal singers were reasonably broad-minded. From a musical

Example 26
Marenzio, 'Scendi dal paradiso'
[Come down from Paradise, O Venus and . . .]

standpoint Marenzio has sacrificed all in a quest for sensuous effect: none of the learnedness of imitative counterpoint, so little dissonance that when it occurs it is all the more striking. Instead, he relies on simple rhythmic cross-accents to convey flightiness of feeling and on a freely varied grouping of voices to give the effect of a dialogue. Much plain block-chordal writing helps to project the words more clearly than in the contrapuntal type of piece.

The publication which marks both the end of his most fecund years as a madrigalist and the beginning of a change in outlook is the *Madrigali à 4, 5, e 6*, book I, of 1588. Its dedication to Count Mario Bevilacqua of Verona, patron of the famous cultural academy there, contains a reference to the new and unorthodox style he had adopted, asserting that he had chosen only texts of deep seriousness. Though resident in Rome, he was a northerner by birth and must always have looked to the north (most of his madrigals were published in Venice), so that it may even be that he was aware of a continuing need for a more serious type of piece in academic circles, although the pastoral madrigal was immensely popular. Certainly the four-part pieces in this collection have an intensity that justifies their consideration being deferred till the next chapter. One of the five-part ones, on the other hand, is still pastoral in feeling, being a setting of a text, *Fiere silvestre*, by Jacopo Sannazzaro, the author of *Arcadia* himself. The wild, sylvan creatures and the sharp, jagged rocks of which it speaks are more than a background for a lover's ardent sighs, they are symbolic of his mood, so it is perhaps a surprise to find that Marenzio treats it lightly and delicately though not without feeling. The word-painting is restrained: a touch of chromaticism, maybe, in the opening bass line, mere 6/3 chords for 'dolore', hardly an anguished intake of breath at 'con si caldi sospir'. But the harmony is warmly coloured, with some good dominant seventh chords, and a remarkable final cadence—D minor first inversion moving to A major. This madrigal does not in any way foretell what was to come in Marenzio's later years.

Nor, for that matter, does the magnificent setting of *Come fuggir*, from Book V *à 6* (1591), which will serve as an excellent representative of Marenzio's handling of this rich texture. That he was fully accustomed to the way of writing for six voices is borne out by his substantial output for the medium—six volumes compared with nine in five parts. As the title implies, the mood of the madrigal aspires to the skies, and is matched by the brilliant scoring for SSAATB in C major with the high clef-range (i.e. the soprano parts lie high in the treble clef and the bass is written in the baritone clef, with mezzo-soprano and alto clefs for alto and tenor voices respectively). It opens with another of Marenzio's rising conjunct themes (as in *Fiere silvestre*), and as if to emphasize the airy feeling the bass is silent for 25 bars until the first cloud appears on the horizon: 'my untamed love does not listen to me'. A quotation of the passage leading up to this entry will show in how masterly a fashion Marenzio controls the rhythmic flow, by having the top part begin with a breve and finally blossom out in 'running' crotchets; notice also the characteristically abrupt change of mood when the bass enters, marked by a touch of chromatics in the beautifully delayed soprano entry (Example 27). The piece thrives on such contrasts between the setting of each short section of text, which are the very stuff of the up-to-date madrigal in Italy.

Let us now for a moment turn back and consider the early career of a composer who stands slightly aside from the development of the lighter madrigals so far discussed in this chapter. Giaches de Wert (1535–96) is distinct in another way: he was the last Franco-Flemish

Example 27
Marenzio, 'Come fuggir'
[O murmur running through the waving grass
Thus my untamed love . . .]

composer to settle in Italy (unlike Lassus or Monte who were there for comparatively brief periods) and to work alongside the native Italians who had now taken the lead in madrigal-writing if not in sacred music. His youth was spent in southern Italy but he achieved fame as *maestro* at the ducal court of the Gonzagas in Mantua from 1565 until his death. Of special interest is his choice of texts for madrigals: he set a greater proportion—68 madrigals in all—of Petrarch than of any

T.M.—C

other writer, second to which in importance came the epic and lyric poems of Ariosto and Torquato Tasso. Wert was in fact the first madrigalist to set Tasso, who was a contemporary and friend at the Mantuan court. Unlike Marenzio, Wert was not inspired to his greatest heights by amorous texts; it was the soul-searching sonnets of Petrarch and other texts of a philosophical or even religious nature which brought out the best in him.[1]

His first madrigal book for five voices appeared in 1558 and showed the influence of Willaert and Rore. In it he employed the motet-like earlier madrigal vein infused with modern elements like remote modulations and false relations, sectional alternations of homophony and polyphony and a feel for tonality. His expressive manner was modelled on that of Rore, for he was not one for the more obvious imitation of nature let alone the crude 'eye music' (black notes for 'night', two semibreves for 'two eyes', etc.—the look of the page being as important as the sound) found in Marenzio's more facile efforts; he preferred lyricism and harmonic colouring, seen in the frequent sequences of 6/3 chords that became one of his mannerisms (e.g. in *Aspro cor*, in Book I, where the idea was suggested in Willaert's setting), or in this restrained opening of *Cantai, or piango* from Book II (1561), where the contrast between singing and weeping is subtly painted (Example 28). These pieces belong to the period before Wert's musical personality was fully matured; his later harmonic experimentation and new ways of handling voices belong properly to the later discussion of Wert the mannerist.

Wert stands, with his Mantuan connections, as a direct link between Rore and Monteverdi. Another who could be viewed thus was the nobleman Alessandro Striggio (c. 1535–87), a Mantuan by birth and connected with both the Gonzaga court and the Medici court at Florence. Einstein describes him as 'anything but a pastoral madrigalist', though as a writer of entertainment music with a fondness for realism and the bizarre (he wrote a seven-part dialogue called *Il cicalamento delle donne al bucato*, 'the chattering of the women at the wash', no doubt the saga of a latter-day laundrette, not to mention *Al vag'e incerto gioco di primiera*, a representation of a card game in music) his name is worthy of mention. His eight-part *Mentre l'un polo*, written for the wedding of Bianca Capello in 1579, is similar in aim and sonority to so many other grandiose wedding madrigals written ever since Corteccia's nine-part *Ingredere*, intended for another Florentine

Example 28
Wert, 'Cantai, or piango'
[I sang, now I weep]

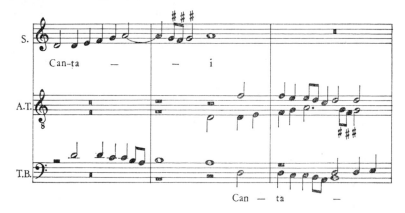

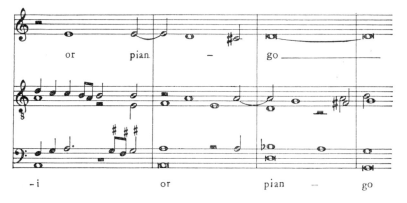

wedding forty years earlier, and can be compared also with Andrea Gabrieli's *Felici d'Adria*.

If Mantua seemed to stand apart in this heyday of the witty pastoral madrigal, what of the rest of northern Italy? Anthologies of this light and artificial music were pouring from the Venetian presses. One of the many 'floridi virtuosi d'Italia'—as contributors to these anthologies were styled—was Lelio Bertani, whose *Ch'ami la vita mia* appeared in a publication dated 1583. We know little of the life of this minor figure, but the madrigal is cleverly wrought, with hints of the *concertato* style in the interweaving of two sopranos over a harmonic bass-line, and some workmanlike contrapuntal variations of contrasted motives towards the end. On the other hand the name of Orazio Vecchi (1550–1605), canon of Correggio cathedral and later *maestro* at the cathedral of Modena, his birthplace, is of considerable significance. He was an inspired master of the light madrigal no matter for what texture it was scored, as well as other forms like the *canzonetta* and also the dramatic madrigal comedy. A typical, expertly composed five-part piece is *Leggiadretto Clorino*, published in 1589. Here the dainty pattering style of declamation is much in evidence, particularly in this central section, introduced by a definite 'modulation' to the dominant area of D minor (the piece is in G minor with frequent digressions of F major) (Example 29). The contrasted quick movement may be carried out in delicate interplay over a sturdy bass-line ('tra le vermiglie rose') or in a descending sequence beneath the independent second soprano line ('giocar saltando') that looks forward to Monteverdi's use of that device. Other parts of the madrigal display Vecchi's contrapuntal skill, which was of a kind no less in demand for the artful presentation of a pastoral madrigal text than for serious church music. But this was counterpoint which, with its strong tonal feeling and harmonic framework, anticipated the *concertato* style, so that the addition of a *basso continuo* strummed on a spinet or plucked on a lute seemed quite a small step. This was one of many ways in which the Baroque had been hinted at years before the turn of the seventeenth century.

The dramatic madrigal comedy was mentioned above: this was a significant development in the last two decades of the sixteenth century, consisting of a complete cycle of madrigals in a dramatic sequence with elements of dialogue between various 'characters'. It grew out of the madrigal-singing tradition of the cultural academies and was for private rather than public entertainment; but its appeal was more on the human level than the learned, high-flown works that had been the usual fare of these bodies in earlier decades. They are prefigured in the large-scale dialogues of Donato and Striggio, where groups of voices are used in conversation, an idea which—but for the use of a single,

Example 29
Vecchi, 'Leggiadretto Clorino'
[Parma observed playing and jumping like a pure flock among the scarlet roses and white flowers]

Parm' all' hor di mi — ra — re Tra

le vermiglie ro — se, Tra le vermiglie ro — se,

Tra le vermiglie ro — se bianchi fio — re Giocar sal —

— tan do, saltan — do, sal — tan — d'un can — did' ar — me — li — no

monodic line for each character—leads on in its turn to the concept
of music-drama or, in other words, opera itself. The madrigal comedy
seen at its best in Vecchi's *L'Amfiparnaso* (1597), represents a true
reflection of the life of the times and contains an amalgam of different
secular styles, uniting within its scope not only madrigal and dialogue
but also the lighter forms both polished and crude, with consequent
folk-like effects at times. Although dramatic in format, it is not an
actual forerunner of *opera buffa*, but it serves the same purpose in the
context of the society it entertained as light opera later did in a different
social environment.

L'Amfiparnaso*, Vecchi's most celebrated work, means literally 'the
two slopes of Parnassus'—comedy and tragedy—and is laid out as a
prologue and three acts. Its text, probably by Vecchi himself, is,
according to Dent, the first existing one of a *commedia dell'arte* play;
certainly some of the characters, such as Pantalone, the Venetian
merchant and Dr Gratiano, the Bolognese doctor, are stock figures
associated with this form of entertainment. In the prologue, the young
lover Lelio introduces the comedy to the audience, likening the world
to a stage and explaining that the spectacle is to be observed with the
mind 'which it enters through the ears, not the eyes': the visual effect
is to be imagined, just as in a radio play. The audience were simply
the friends of the five singers seated round the music-room. This is
why there is no monophonic representation of characters as a rule
(the opening of Act I is an exception) not even, say, a consistent use of
lower voices to represent male characters like Pantalone. Vecchi's
humour consists in burlesquing Italian dialects and also current musical
styles, whether that of sacred polyphony or of the low *villanella* with
its rustic consecutive fifths (e.g. Hortensia's stuttering self-introduction).
The vocal writing is excellently varied so that we can always follow
the drama, and one agrees with Dent how lively and full-blooded it
all is compared with the anaemic recitation of Peri's *Euridice*, the first
opera.[2]

The *Convito Musicale*, also published in 1597, is less a madrigal
comedy than a 'musical feast' of light madrigals in his best brilliant
style, showing the *rapprochement* with the *canzonetta*. A notable
technique, exemplified well in the high-voiced central section of
Fummo felici, is the treatment of two pairs of voices as if they were two
separated choirs passing the same short phrase between them to
produce a hypnotic harmonic effect (Example 30). It is however, a

tame way to set the words 'holds shame still burning for my love neglected'.

The other important madrigal comedy writer was the Bolognese Adriano Banchieri who, for a Benedictine monk, seemed to get well involved in the scintillating social life of that city. Its academies, while still cultural in pursuit, were more interested in entertainment than in propagating revolutionary theories about monody, as the Florentine Camerata did, and Banchieri's delightful *Festino nella sera del giovedì grasso* (1608) contains, among other worldly attractions, an imitation

Example 30
Vecchi, 'Fummo felici'
[Holds shame (still burning) for my love neglected]

of a cuckoo, owl, cat and dog improvising a 'bestial counterpoint' over a *cantus firmus*.

All this could be grouped under Einstein's label 'music in company', for it was not staged. Another form of entertainment music was that performed at big court events—the *intermedii* staged between acts of a play, during scene changes, to delight a much grander audience. From a musical standpoint this was closely related in function and style to the ceremonial wedding madrigals we have encountered from time to time, but in another way it proved important as a precursor for opera, particularly as it was accompanied by just the visual effects— ballets, allegorical tableaux and so on—that were to form a significant part of early Baroque opera. Fortunately the complete music and documentation for one very grand event, the marriage in 1589 of Ferdinando de' Medici and Cristina of Lorraine at Florence, has been edited in a modern edition.[3] Its relevance here is in showing us how Marenzio, the only madrigalist who contributed, faced the task of writing music for a complete *intermedio*. There is an opening *sinfonia* for instruments followed by madrigals *à 3, 6, 12* and *18*. With scenery and costumes to match, this must have been one of the most sumptuous entertainments in an age that sought to be sensually uplifted, whether in the frivolous music of the madrigal or in the massive ear-tickling stereophony of multichoral Venetian church music.

1. C. MacClintock, 'Some Notes on the Secular Music of Giaches de Wert', *Musica Disciplina*, x (1956), p. 106.

2. *New Oxford History of Music*, iv (London, 1968), p. 77.

3. D. P. Walker, *Les Fêtes du Mariage* . . . (Paris, 1963).

5

MANNERISM AND THE LATE
ITALIAN MADRIGAL

The style of the pastoral madrigal and its great popularity, both in Italy and abroad, represents only one aspect of the later Italian madrigal. In the last decades of the sixteenth century a *rapprochement* was taking place between the pastoral and the lighter forms of secular music, which we shall view in more detail in the following chapter, and at the same time there appeared a more definite distinction between such lighter music and the much deeper and more intense works of Marenzio and Wert in their later life, and of Gesualdo throughout his career. From these it is but a short step to the early madrigals of Monteverdi: his inclusion in the present chapter is not intended to imply that he wrote no pastoral madrigals, but to show how the roots of his style lie in the 'mannerist' phase of the Italian madrigal.

This phase is characterized not only by seriousness of mood—reflected in the way that more profound types of text now find greater appeal with composers—but also by a new virtuosity in the voice-writing. The ensembles for which these madrigals were in general conceived were not merely groups of reasonably capable amateurs, who could do justice, for example, to most of Marenzio's early works, but really gifted groups associated with cultural academies whose singers might be professional in attainment if not by occupation, or indeed groups made up of professional court singers in cities like Ferrara and Mantua, which were able to attract some of the greatest talents of the day. Whereas up till now the stylistic growth of the madrigal had not been confined to one small geographical area, in this late phase most of the important activity took place in north Italy, and especially in the two cities just mentioned. Even though Marenzio remained in Rome, his later madrigals were spiritually of the North. Thus it is not only in the field of sacred music but also in that of the madrigal that northern Italy is the key area where the transition from the late Renaissance to the Baroque is wrought.

The use of the word 'mannerism' in connection with the late madrigal calls for some explanation. This term, though a comparative late-comer into the field of musical history, has long been accepted in the history of art and architecture, not merely to label one short phase or generation, but as a complete period coming between Renaissance and Baroque, and lasting from about 1530 to 1600. Though by no means consistently interpreted by critics, a possible definition of a mannerist is one who is preoccupied by problems of style for its own sake and who thus indulges in artificiality. Viewed this way, and bearing in mind the dates of the mannerist epoch, it is tempting to agree with John Shearman[1] that, as a musical manifestation, the entire phenomenon of the Italian madrigal fills the bill very conveniently. And he has a point: for indeed it seems to form a self-sufficient entity in musical history, and nobody could deny that artificiality and convention are present throughout its heyday. Unlike sacred music, in which the liturgical text is a timeless peg on which to hang the music, the madrigal is associated with a literary movement which conforms to mannerist ideas and is developed in those centres where mannerist art flourished.

This is, however, too generalized a view, for it postulates the complete detachment of the Italian madrigal from the rest of musical development in the late Renaissance, and at the same time smooths over the very important changes of emphasis within its own growth. Let us look once again at the proposed definition of mannerism: a preoccupation with problems of style. This entails the emphasis on details at the expense of the whole; whereas a Renaissance painting or building has a natural poise and symmetry, the mannerist one may draw attention to its details by a deliberate avoidance of these qualities, by stark contrasts and even by distortions. An example of this can be seen in the studied imbalance of the architecture of Michelangelo's Medici Chapel at Florence, or in some of his sculptures. It is just these features that typify the later serious madrigal. Artificiality of itself is not enough: Palestrina's counterpoint is, in the best sense of the term, artificial, as are many of the light, pastoral madrigals, but neither of these genres belong to true mannerist art. If we remember that the other school of composers to whom the term 'mannerist' has been applied was the group of late fourteenth-century French chanson writers whose preoccupation was extreme rhythmic and notational complexity, we can assert that mannerist phases can be expected to occur towards the end of major historical periods. *Fin de siècle* tendencies are inherent in every artistic development, as the styles are worked out, and it is no surprise to find that mannerism affected not sacred music but the madrigal, where more freedom of expression prevailed.

Of all the details to which a mannerist could draw attention in music, none strikes the listener more forcibly than chromaticism. We have already seen how the word itself is derived from 'colour', so that as a musical device it could be compared with the artist's use of various unusual or intense tints in a painting. An unusual leap in a voice part may be concealed by the polyphonic texture; a chromatic passage, however short, is immediately striking since it affects both the line and the vertical harmonies. Composers and theorists had of course been experimenting with chromaticism since the 1520s, and Rore had incorporated it into his mature madrigals without sacrificing restraint. It is no accident that Rore and other experimenters were all connected with Ferrara, and that this was also the home of one who provides a historical link between Rore and Gesualdo in the use of new modes of expression: Luzzasco Luzzaschi.

Luzzaschi (d. 1607) had in fact been a pupil of Rore's during the latter's period in Ferrara and became first organist at the court chapel of Duke Alfonso II; in his turn he was to teach the great organist Frescobaldi. His madrigal publications span the period from 1570 or so till his death, and even in quite early works he was already expressing himself in an individual, mannerist idiom. We shall encounter his fascinating monodies with keyboard accompaniment later; it is as a precursor of Gesualdo that he concerns us here. Suffice it to say that the solo pieces were written for a trio of highly talented sopranos who came to be known as the 'three ladies of Ferrara', and that with their remarkably ornate style they fit into the picture of the professional madrigal conceived with virtuoso performers in mind. One of Luzzaschi's most well-known five-part madrigals is *Quivi sospiri*, from his second book (1576); the text is one of the few by Dante—from the *Inferno*—that was ever set. The chromaticism is largely of a linear kind, but despite the fact that it is more controlled than in Gesualdo, it represents a very bold conception for this date. Particularly notice-

able too, is Luzzaschi's tendency to break up the phrases with rests
(Example 31). This gasping effect anticipates Gesualdo, as also does
Luzzaschi's predilection for indefinite cadences at the ends of madrigals:
neither *Quivi sospiri* nor the two pieces Einstein quotes in Vol. III of
The Italian Madrigal end with obvious cadences. *Quivi sospiri* and
Itene mie querele both finish on Phrygian cadences which are rendered
vague by the troubled harmonies that precede them. The latter madrigal is very close to the later style of Gesualdo, who may indeed have
modelled his setting of *Itene o miei sospiri* upon it, as we shall see.

And so we come to that unique figure Gesualdo himself. Carlo

Example 31
Luzzaschi, 'Quivi sospiri'
[Shrill, weak voices]

Gesualdo da Venosa (*c.* 1560–1613) was a Neapolitan and an aristocrat,
who in 1585 succeeded to the house of Gesualdo—an event which
forced him into an unhappy first marriage that later drove him to
murder his wife and her lover. In the last decade of the century he
travelled in north Italy, settling in Ferrara from 1594 until Duke
Alfonso's II's death, after which he returned to Naples. His pathological
neurotic personality, which has fascinated his biographers, found its
psychological outlet in his six volumes of five-part madrigals published between 1594 and 1611 and written, it seems, more for personal
expression than for actual singers. His intimate friendship with Tasso,
the court poet at Ferrara who so inspired Wert, links him with the
mannerist circle despite his southern origins.

Gesualdo should not be viewed as an innovator: the expressionist
element in his music has a precedent in Marenzio, and the tendency
to break the flow by rests in all the voices, the quest for an epigrammatic brevity, is prefigured in Luzzaschi, who was the most important
formative influence. In the field of chromaticism Gesualdo proceeded

from Luzzaschi's style and pushed his experiments to *fin de siècle* extremes, so that his last madrigals produce an effect of 'musical seasickness' (Einstein's phrase). In other respects, he was distinctly conservative: at a time when new ways of exploiting a five-part texture were being tried out by Wert and Monteverdi which were to lead to its final demise, Gesualdo's idiom remained rooted in a linear, equal-voiced polyphony; at a time when instrumental accompaniment was becoming more common and only a few years would elapse before Monteverdi was combining voices and instruments in the big *concertato* madrigal, Gesualdo stuck to the vocal medium, for the letters of his courtly attendant tell us nothing about instrumental participation. He was cautious in his use of homophony and the clear vertical thinking associated with it, and made no play with two equal upper voices over a harmonic type of bass-line, such a forward-looking feature of Marenzio's work. Neither did the monodic style have any effect upon him, even though he employed Francesco Rasi, one of Caccini's best pupils, for two years, and cannot therefore have been ignorant of its existence.[2]

As with Marenzio and Wert, Gesualdo's mannerism does not emerge fully until the later works. In the earlier madrigals his harmonic progressions create a wayward feeling rather than a wild and passionate one. As yet there are none of the really violent juxtapositions of fast and slow motion that are so prominent later on, and the angularity of individual melodic lines does not seem to be harnessed to dramatic effect. Maturity comes in his Book IV (1596) and is well illustrated by the first piece in the volume, *Luci serene e chiare*. Here chromatics are used with restraint, their full impact being reserved for the very last words 'more e non langue'. There is a structural coherence in the alternation of slow chordal and excited imitative strains, laid out in a clear AA'BB' form with the B sections having the same text. Each musical section is thus subtly varied upon repeat, and Gesualdo loses no opportunity for a more pungent expression by slight alterations of the part writing (Example 32).

The madrigals of Book V (1611) show how such harmonic asperity —to which chromatics are not always essential—comes to dominate Gesualdo's dissonance technique, and to be reserved to the slower, 'depressive' phase of a piece, exaggerating the contrast between these and the 'manic' music of the faster interludes. That this contrast had already been tried out by Luzzaschi can be seen by comparing his

Example 32
Gesualdo, 'Luci serene e chiare'
[Longing and not grieving]

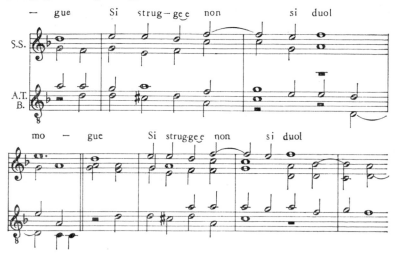

Itene mie querele, mentioned earlier, and Gesualdo's *Itene o miei sospiri*: it is the most striking feature of the opening of both pieces. Gesualdo has added the obvious 'gasping' effect for 'sospiri', but has almost plagiarized Luzzaschi's 'precipitate' with the appropriate tumbling melodic line. Their respective approaches to the plea 'ditele per pietà' are subtly different; though both are sequential (a device which helps to maintain equilibrium in such troubled music) Gesualdo's falling bass and suspension seems to lack the confidence of Luzzaschi's bold rising fourths in the bass (Example 33). Both paint the 'change to joy' near the end with a change to triple time but only for a brief moment, and Gesualdo's rather confused contrapuntal conclusion contrasts with his forbear's strong chordal finish. In the terms of his style, his progressions have a certain sense of direction, even though an unexpected sting in the tail may confound the listener's expectations. In another madrigal from Book V, *Dolcissima mia vita*, Gesualdo is more concerned with chromatic movements in individual parts, which may stand out prominently against a static harmony (bars 21–2) or, as at the remarkable ending, be combined in a fragmentary contrapuntal texture (Example 34). This represents the ultimate development of linear chromaticism, and though the technique of

Example 33 (a)
Luzzaschi, 'Itene mie querele'
[Say it, out of pity]

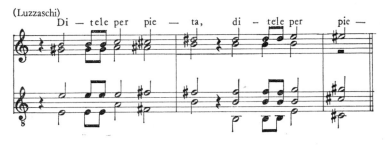

(Luzzaschi)
Di — tele per   pie — ta,   di — tele per   pie —

Example 33 (b)
Gesualdo, 'Itene o miei sospiri'
[Say it, out of pity]

(Gesualdo)

Di — .tele   per pie-tà   di — tele   per   pietà

contrary motion in bars 43–4 looks forward to the atonal writing of
Schönberg, it shows that Gesualdo was at heart a linear composer. The
essence of his style does not lie in the prophetic harmonic progressions
(e.g. the opening of *Moro lasso al mio duolo* from Book VI) which
modern commentators have seized upon, with their grand retrospective view of the rise and fall of tonality. His harmonic eccentricity
led him up a cul-de-sac; his melodic avenues were to be avidly explored
by the monodists.

If the mannerist element in Gesualdo is almost entirely represented
by dissonance in general and chromaticism in particular, in the later
works of Marenzio and Wert it takes on more diverse and less blatant
forms, of which chromaticism is only an incidental one. The madrigal-
buying public were aware of the changes of style, for both composers'
later volumes achieved far less popularity in the form of numerous
reprintings than their earlier ones.

First, what use did Marenzio make of chromaticism? He had been

Example 34
Gesualdo, 'Dolcissima mia vita'
[O to die]

aware of the powers of expression that it afforded from his earliest works, as we can see from this false relation (A, TII) and chromatic movement in the alto at the end of *Dolorosi martir* (Example 35). Even such slight touches could bring forth moments of heart-rending expression. There is also the celebrated enharmonic modulation in *O voi che sospirate*[3] which shows an awareness of equal temperament; the words here speak of 'change . . . his ancient song', inviting Marenzio to parody the music of the ancients by an excursion into the enharmonic *genera* of the Greeks by which the theorists were then fascinated.

Example 35
Marenzio, 'Dolorosi martir'
[Every bitter absence]

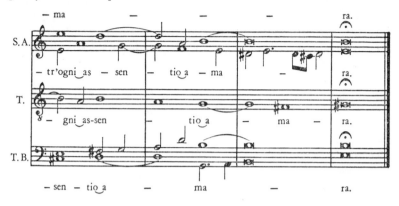

In later works Marenzio used chromatic modulations with more telling effect. In *O fere stelle*, for instance, he establishes a firm Dorian G minor mode from which the music modulates in a flatwards direction to a clear cadence in D♭, and later in a sharpward one to reach a chord of B major, the climax of a chain of slow-moving harmonies. But perhaps the most extraordinary example of chromaticism occurs in a very late work, *Solo e pensoso*, published in the eleventh book of five-part madrigals (1599, the year of his death) dedicated to Duke Vincenzo Gonzaga of Mantua and appropriately called his most Mantuan set.[4] The gloom of Marenzio's last years is captured in Petrarch's words, which depict a solitary wanderer detached from everyday life, and the music reflects this scene exactly—a slow, aimless succession of semibreves rising and falling through the chromatic scale, entirely detached from the angular polyphony below it.

Let us now examine more general manifestations of Marenzio's change away from the lightly-painted, beautifully wrought madrigals that had so delighted the public in his first few books. The change is felt no less in four-part madrigals than in those for more conventional textures, so that the setting of *Se la mia vita* (1588) makes a good comparison with the four-part *Chi vuol'udir'* of four years earlier, referred to in the last chapter. Petrarch's words have the undercurrent of death that seemed to fascinate Marenzio more and more in his later years:

If my life continues in spite of bitter torment and pain,
so that in my final years, lady, the radiance of your
eyes is gone . . .

The madrigal is in two sections, both of which with almost motet-like
imitative entries; but the effect is not that of a madrigalist who only
knows a conventional motet idiom, like the lesser Roman figures of
the time; it breathes a deliberate austerity entirely in keeping with the
text. Where the conventional church composer turning his hand to
madrigals would preserve a more even harmonic flow, Marenzio
soon infuses a feeling of anguish into the music: bass suspensions for

Example 36
Marenzio, 'Se la mia vita'
[Fearful and slow]

'dall'aspro tormento', or a surprising chord of B♭ which is outside the
mode (bars 54 and 167), the second of which is most dramatic coming
so soon after a D major cadence, or—prophetic chord, if you like—an
actual diminished seventh at bar 98 (Example 36). Not for nothing
did Arnold call Marenzio 'the Schubert of the madrigal'.

Despite these events, this madrigal preserves a motet-like feeling in
its reluctance to surprise the listener with dramatic changes of expression or to abandon a continuous flow. Marenzio was capable of
maintaining such austerity right up to his last book of madrigals (1599),
by relying on unusual leaps and complex dissonance treatment to
give a mannerist intensity. In the remarkable setting of *Crudele acerba*
from this book there is not a single general pause in all the voices of
the kind that features so often in Gesualdo, and scarcely any deviations
of tempo from the relentless minim beat compared to Gesualdo's
restless alterations of speed, and yet in this very continuity lies the
power to build up tension and relax it. For a madrigal that relies more
upon a disjunct succession of ideas we return to *Solo e pensoso*, whose
chromatic opening has already been mentioned. The melodic lines

sometimes have an aimless quality, false relations arising almost inconsequentially, and even a chordal passage ('altro scherno') seems to lack direction because of its emphasis on minor chords. When the lines adopt a more purposeful attitude, their shape is exaggerated and their rhythms made more jerky, just as in a mannerist painting. Even a group of mellifluous 6/3 chords in parallel motion is interrupted by an unexpected chord on 'perché' (why?). This is a madrigal of contrast and asymmetry, for the opening chromatic passage stands alone and there is hardly anything but purely innocuous harmonic writing thereafter. In this way it differs utterly from *Crudele acerba*.

Marenzio's dedication of this book of madrigals to the Duke of Mantua and their actual style link his work to that of the two great Mantuans, Wert and Monteverdi, reminding us that it was in this city that the Italian madrigal received the final impetus which propelled it into the seventeenth century. Of all the famous ruling families residing in north Italian cities, the Gonzagas, through the progressive and organized rule of Duke Guglielmo, brought great names into contact with court culture, with the result that its composers were second only to those in Rome or Venice. True, Ferrara was still associated with progressive ideas, and though this was to come to an end in 1598 with the transference of the d'Este court to nearby Modena, Wert maintained his connections with the city by involving himself in a tragic love-affair with Tarquinia Molza, one of the famous 'three ladies', by his friendship with Tasso, the court poet there, and by composing for the *Accademia degli Intrepidi*. Such connections, by bringing him into contact with Ferrara's tradition of experiment, undoubtedly led to the more modern outlook that we can see from his seventh book of madrigals (1581) onwards. But it is as a Mantuan that Wert became known to Monteverdi, and proved to be the one who influenced him most. In order to show this more strongly, it is best to have deferred till now a study of Wert's later output even though mannerist tendencies were apparent in it as early as 1581.

The full flowering of his maturity can be seen in this seventh book of madrigals, and since one madrigal, on the already-familiar Petrarch text *Solo e pensoso*, exhibits so many marks of his later style, we should turn our attention to it first. From the very outset the most striking feature is the eccentricity of the vocal lines: the bass part has the most extreme example, with not only the two successive falling fifths of the imitation point, but also two successive rising sixths and a fall of a tenth forming part of a descent through almost two octaves! This type of vocal writing becomes for Wert one of the most characteristic means of mannerist expression in these later works. After such an extraordinary opening Wert provides the strongest contrast for the next line of text 'vo misurando a passi tardi', this measured tread being represented by the smoothest conjunct lines and rising sequences, culminating at bars 51–53 in a quite archaic cadence-formula of the kind that he would have learned from his Franco-Flemish predecessors, for this could almost be Josquin. Such contrapuntal usages are frequent in Wert—they can be seen again in the beautiful bass suspension of bar 66 or the contrary motion of the alto in bars 86–88—and are used for expressive ends as well as for their polyphonic brilliance. After bar 53 the tempo of the madrigal increases speed, never to regain the slow, contemplative tread of the opening: here, then, is an asymmetry of tempo, just as in Marenzio's setting there is asymmetry in the use of chromaticism.

Wert's harmonies are quite straightforward in themselves, though sometimes eccentric in juxtaposition, as at the end of the *prima parte*, where A♭ major (bar 105) is quickly followed by D major (bar 108). The *seconda parte* of *Solo e pensoso* is notable in exemplifying two devices which, like his unusual melodic spans, form an indispensable part of the late Wert style: parallel 6/3 chords in three voices, and choral recitation on repeated harmonies, almost like a harmonized chanting. 'Parallel 6/3 chords' is maybe a misleading description for their first use in this madrigal, which occurs at a multiple melisma for three voices at once, in flowing quavers most appropriate to the word 'fiumi' (rivers), and so much more brilliant than a conventional single melisma. At their second appearance (bar 147 ff.) their harmonic colour is more deliberately exploited: here the lines leap about in such a way that all sense of harmonic progression is forestalled and the listener is forced to concentrate on each individual harmony, linked by completely non-functional leaps. This passage is skilfully dovetailed into the setting of the final line, which concludes with choral recitation on a repeated chord and lacks any definite form of final cadence.

That all these marks of style are typical can be seen in their frequent appearances in many other madrigals. A better example of choral recitation occurs in *Giunto alla tomba* (also Book VII), where it captures the gloom of the text by means of the low scoring (Example 37). Such fastidious attention to the declamation of the text had a precedent

Example 37
Wert, 'Giunto alla tomba'
[Deprived of colour, of heat, of movement
 The face already having a marble aspect]

in Willaert's *Musica Nova* of 1559, and Wert would also have been aware that the Greek theorists, whose ideas were being resuscitated, emphasized its importance. Many of his later pieces are full of such *parlando* effects. The 6/3 chords turn up equally often, either moving quickly and deftly painting one word, or slowly and conveying pathos, as at the opening of *Crudele acerba*, the effect here being heightened by suspensions and leaps (Example 38).

As for chromaticism, Wert uses it more sparingly, and with less novelty of effect than Marenzio. Where it does occur, it is closely linked with a particular line of text in the conventional manner of Rore, and is handled with the same restraint and concern for symmetry. We can see this in two instances from Book IX of his five-part madrigals (1588): in *Crudele acerba* the words 'and left me here to spend my life in weeping' are set to a simple rising and falling chromatic phrase which, used only in linear fashion, does not bring about any modulation. In the second example, at the end of *Ecco ch'un altra volta*, the chromaticism is even more restricted—to three notes on the word 'lagrime'—and is presented in a diatonic context as part of an imitation point in F major, or as one voice in a harmonic progression even more

Example 38
Wert, 'Crudele acerba'
[Cruel, bitter, inexorable death]

firmly rooted in this key. In both instances it serves merely as a touch of colour at a suitable moment, which is far removed from the Gesualdo concept of chromaticism as an essential ingredient of style.

The element of virtuosity is particularly strong in Wert's Book VIII (1586), which contains the madrigals presumably intended for the three ladies of Ferrara: the three uppermost parts are often brilliantly written. They become detached from the two lowest (*Usciva omai*, for instance, opens with a high C major triad for them), which not only splits the five-part texture down the middle but also gives special prominence to the tenor part. This voice may often introduce a new idea (at bar 50 of *Misera, non credea* Wert places its entry above all the upper voices), or stand rhythmically apart in a chordal passage, as indeed it does in Example 37. There is thus a growing tendency towards inequality which culminates eventually in the madrigal *Ah, dolente partita* (Book XI, 1595), described by Einstein as 'an aria in madrigal guise'. No doubt he refers to the way the top part is from time to time detached and placed in dialogue, or in opposition, to the others. Having started off with the homogeneous texture of Rore in early life, Wert's later predilection for fragmenting it for dramatic ends did much to bring about the textural disintegration of Monteverdi's madrigals. His love of contrast is also apparent in the simultaneous combination of disjunct and conjunct lines, or motives of fast and slow tread, exemplified in this same madrigal, for despite his leanings towards homophonic declamation he remained a contrapuntist to the end.

Such musical devices enhanced rather than detracted from his ability to create a mood. Here too, he had grown away from Rore's detailed approach to word painting (though words like 'notte' or 'pianto' would always draw forth a touch of colour) and developed the consistent view of a whole text, whether it be in the woodland atmosphere suggested by Ariosto's text *Vaghi boschetti*, or the stormier sea-imagery of Sannazzaro's *Ecco ch'un altra volta*. To this new realism, as also to his development of choral declamation and contrapuntal virtuosity, Monteverdi was to owe much.

Claudio Monteverdi (1567–1643) was born at Cremona, another north Italian city somewhat further west than Mantua and Ferrara and certainly much less in touch with modern developments. Here his teacher was Ingegneri, a competent but conventional composer of sacred music and madrigals, happy in the latter field to follow Rore in expressing the words without interrupting the musical flow, in using chromatics without breaking down tonality. To him, as Einstein says, Monteverdi owed virtually nothing. Monteverdi's first book of madrigals (1587) has the charm and delicacy of Marenzio's earlier work, without lacking moments of more passionate expression: it represents what Einstein would call the 'post-classic' style, compared with which the next two volumes come under the mannerist influence of Wert, for, in about 1590, Monteverdi was appointed a member of the orchestra at the Gonzaga court in Mantua, where Wert had for many years been *maestro di cappella*. Monteverdi was to remain in Mantua till 1613, later becoming a singer and finally *maestro* himself in 1601. Working under Wert completely transformed his style into something bold and daring, not perhaps as eccentric as that of late Wert but certainly demanding the same virtuosity from the singers. A fine example of his already assured handling of the medium in the third book (1592) is the setting of Guarini's *O com'è gran martire*. The long opening for a trio of upper voices is exactly like passages in Wert's Book VIII, and once again suggests the three ladies of Ferrara; the clear enunciation of the text recalls Wert, too, and the expressive falling sixth interval, though it became characteristic of Monteverdi, originated in the same source. On the other hand the careful attention to structural balance, polyphonic variety, and vocal colouring have more in common with the best in Marenzio. Monteverdi has clearly grasped how to vary his material (compare, for example, bars 26–30 and 34–41) and to extend a paragraph either by pitting two contrasted motives against each other in a variety of vocal scorings (bars 41–58) or by making one contrapuntal tag gradually take over the musical argument from another (bar 58 to the end).

Book IV (1603) represents the culmination of Monteverdi's early madrigal achievement. Both this and Book III were reprinted several times, unlike the mannerist collections of Wert and Marenzio, though (especially in Book IV) no pains are spared in expressing Guarini's often intense texts. That extravagant erotic expostulation *Si ch'io vorrei morire* lives, or rather dies, by its naked use of dissonance to create tension and relaxation, though even here the emotional ebb and flow does not preclude musical devices such as the return of the opening strain at the end—superbly placed so as to make the climax of the madrigal—or the repetition of the brilliant tutti 'a questo bianco seno', off-setting the falling or rising 'deh stringetemi' idea. In his setting of Rinuccini's *Sfogava con le stelle*, Monteverdi takes Wert's technique of

Example 39
Monteverdi, 'Sfogava con le stelle'
[You do it, yes, with your noble semblance of pity]

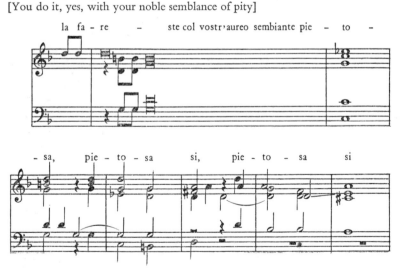

Example 40 (a) and (b)
Monteverdi, 'Cruda Amarilli'
[Alas, a bitter lesson]

choral declamation to its logical conclusion. This is the use of *falso
bordone*, a conventional enough device for psalm-chanting in church
which takes on a new meaning in the context of the madrigal: the
words are underlaid to a single chord and chanted in speech rhythm,
with a resolution in measured music, just as in Anglican chant; but
look at some of the dissonances that follow these resolutions (Example

39). They arise through the movement of unremarkable individual lines—in fact the last two phrases in the top part become a cliché of recitative style in the ensuing decades—but it is their type of irregular harmonic combination that so annoyed a pedantic theorist of the time by the name of Artusi. This man published an attack called *Delle imperfezioni della moderna musica* in 1600, citing in particular several instances of unprepared dominant sevenths in Monteverdi's madrigals. In riposte, Monteverdi justified himself through the mouthpiece of his brother Giulio Cesare in a long preface to his fifth book of madrigals (1605), invoking the whole development of the madrigal towards a concern for expressing the text even at the expense of musical proprieties—what he called the *seconda prattica* or 'second practice'. This subservience of music to text he contrasted with the 'first practice', where the opposite prevailed, as in the sacred polyphony of the Franco-Flemish school.[5]

How complete was the emancipation of the dominant seventh from being one of many passing or suspended dissonances to becoming a functional chord in its own right is illustrated in these examples from *Cruda Amarilli*, the very madrigal of which Artusi complained (Example 40). Neither did he take to the diminished triad in bar 21, though what better a way to lead into the bitter chain of suspensions on 'amaramente'? This madrigal comes from Book V, whose preface expounds the *seconda prattica*, and although Monteverdi's brother was at pains to point out that this was not a new style, Claudio's assurance and genius had by now led the madrigal past the point of no return and grown out of *fin de siècle* mannerism, for these pieces are of the seventeenth century as well as in it. Even if *Cruda Amarilli* was one of the madrigals in Book V that did not require a *basso continuo*, others did; but that is for a later chapter.

1. J. Shearman, *Mannerism* (London, 1967), p. 96 ff.

2. A. Newcomb, 'Carlo Gesualdo and a Musical Correspondence of 1594', *The Musical Quarterly*, liv (1968), p. 409.

3. Quoted in D. Arnold, *Marenzio* (London, 1965), pp. 14–15.

4. ibid., p. 36.

5. Artusi's attack and this riposte are printed in O. Strunk, *Source Readings in Music History* (New York, 1950), pp. 393 ff.

6

THE LIGHTER FORMS:

THE SPIRITUAL MADRIGAL

Throughout the successive waves of the Italian madrigal's development there existed a parallel on a more popular plane in the shape of the *villanella*, later replaced by the *canzonetta*, and its kindred forms. The full name of the *villanella* during its early heyday was *canzon villanesca alla napoletana*, signifying that it was of Neapolitan origin; this heyday occurred almost as soon as the madrigal in the north began to part company with the erstwhile popular frottola style, so that, even if it was southern in spirit, it could be seen to fill a new vacuum that had been left in the field of humbler secular music. It was a less polished, more folk-like counterpart to the madrigal, to which it stood in opposition—not the opposition implied in 'class distinction' between aristocracy and peasants but that implied in the present-day difference between classical and 'pop'. In general, the lighter forms provided entertainment music at a time when the madrigal had become an elevated cultural activity concerned more with intellectual speculation than convivial jollification.

The *villanella* was less similar in function to the frottola than to its related genre, the carnival song, for it was often connected with special entertainments in costume performed on days of celebration. In one guise it was known as the *villotta*, whose origins were in street cries full of nonsense syllables and which dated back to the fifteenth century. This later became simplified into the *mascherata*, a staged piece sung in costume by groups of three singers and therefore set to easily memorable music.

Little is known of the lives of the early Neapolitans who wrote *villanelle*. The two most important were Giovan Tommaso di Maio and Gian Domenico da Nola; a lesser figure was Tommaso Cimello. Unlike the frottola, which had been a four-part composition, the *villanella* was scored for three voices in close harmony. A liberal sprinkling of consecutive fifths in the form of root-position triads added to the primitive, barbarous elements in the music, as in this opening from one of Maio's pieces, *Tutte le vecchie* (Example 41). As Einstein says, these fifths were at first purely rustic, but their use later

Example 41
Maio, 'Tutte le vecchie'
[All old women are malicious]

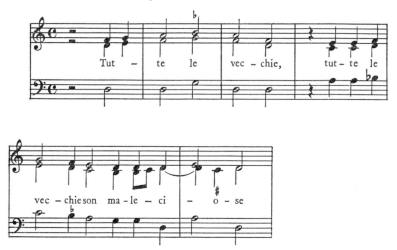

became an increasingly self-conscious means of demonstrating against the 'rules' and the technical mastery of the serious madrigal.[1] This aggressive spirit would certainly be found in Nola's work, for he was perfectly capable of writing serious madrigals in four and five parts,[2] some of which he published in 1564 (his *Canzone villanesche* had appeared in the early 1540s, Maio's in 1546). Like most other forms of light music, not excluding the present-day 'pop' song, the *villanella* was strophic, and there was therefore no question of such subtleties as word painting.

On the other hand there could be, within certain limits, some variety in different types of *villanella*. Those of Nola seem to fall into two styles. There are the very simple chordal pieces, probably performed in costume from memory, like the song of the blind men, *Tre ciechi siamo*, croaking their way through a combination of serenading and begging. This excerpt shows one minute concession to ornament, some

Example 42
Nola, 'Tre ciechi siamo'
[O beautiful ladies have pity
 Be charitable to the deprived
 Give some alms to us poor wretches]

nice fifths, and the drunken stagger of the rhythms with their unorthodox groupings and time-changes (Example 42). These songs often begin 'we are blind men/doctors/adventurers, etc.', continue with propositions that are sometimes unprintable and certainly make play with the *double entendre*. The other type are the less bawdy, more soulful lovers' laments which have more independence in the vocal writing and a poise and balance in their melodies. In this opening of *Madonn'io*

Example 43
Nola, 'Madonn'io non lo so'
[My lady, I know not why you do it]

non lo so there is a particularly enticing syncopation in bar 5, and although the tune consists of two exact repetitions of a four-bar phrase, the lower voices are cleverly varied (Example 43). Nola also wrote a delightful non-strophic piece, *Chichilichi*, which is an example of the *moresca*, a form which parodies, among other things, the madrigal street ballad, African folklore and spoken gibberish. This is a dialogue between two Negro damsels on the subject of their amorous experiences simply set to music but brilliantly brought off. Like all the other pieces it was intended to amuse both the Neapolitans and the Venetians.

And indeed the *villanella* quickly caught on up in the north: Nola's publications were printed at Venice, and Willaert himself was quick to enter the field with his *Canzone villanesche à 4* of 1545. But these were in four parts, not three; with Willaert's contribution to the genre there appears a parting of the ways between the rustic regional type with a genuine folk-like spirit and the more respectable four-part composition with its leanings towards the madrigal. In fact Willaert's four-part pieces are more closely related to the superseded frottola in their texture. Even an almost entirely homophonic one like *O bene mio*, despite its clear and simple AABCC structure, has a sophistication of rhythm and harmony removed from the realm of the street song. Others have a measure of interplay between the voices that suggests a light madrigal. Willaert merely used Nola's *villanelle* as a starting point; in some cases he put Nola's tunes in his tenor part and added three new parts. In his rearrangement of *Madonn'io non lo so* (Example 43) he manages to preserve the raciness of Nola's music and adds a delightful syncopation in his 'descant' in bars 4 and 8, whilst extending Nola's bar 5 syncopation to all parts other than the tenor tune (Example 44). An example of madrigal-like respectability of style is afforded in *Zoia zentil*, a piece with a text in Venetian dialect, which displays the artful device of presenting a *fa-la*-type refrain homophonically and then varying it contrapuntally, and also has some pair contrasts to relieve the continuous four-part texture. Another Venetian who took to rearranging Nola's *villanelle* in the same way was Perissone Cambio, in whose setting of Nola's *Oyme oyme* the original simplicity is rather more overlaid with independent part writing: Cambio was, like Willaert, primarily a madrigalist.

Now that the serious madrigal had, by the 1550s, adopted the five-part medium as standard, the four-part one was generally used for the popular forms in the north. A typical mid-century collection was the

Example 44
Willaert, 'Madonn'io non lo so'
[My lady, I know not why you do it]

Canzone villanesche (c. 1550) by yet another Venetian, Baldassare Donato, which proved popular enough to be reprinted in 1556. The style varies between the absolutely chordal, where dance-like rhythms are the main attraction (e.g. *Viva sempre in ogn'estate*), and the contrapuntally varied. *Chi la gagliarda* is a delightful example of the latter sort, a kind of sixteenth-century 'invitation to the dance': the lusty men are so keen to dance their galliard with the maidens that the

Example 45
Donato, 'Chi la gagliarda'
[Come to us, the excellent masters]

music momentarily breaks into triple time against the basic duple beat (Example 45). In fact even this *villanella* does not prove to be an entirely original conception: for if we look at Nola's setting of the same text we find that all Donato's rhythms are the same. He does not pirate any of Nola's melodies (except at the opening) or harmonies, he simply proceeds from his rhythmic patterns and extends them on to a larger scale. And the consecutive fifths of Nola's jolly refrain 'tan tan tan tantira' would stick out in Donato's polished idiom, though the nonsense syllables survive in a new setting.

It may surprise us to realize that Orlandus Lassus was a very distinguished contributor to the repertory of the *villanella*. During his period in Italy in the 1540s and '50s he was no doubt attracted, especially on a visit to Naples, to its style of popular music, for in 1555 he published a first book of *Madrigali villanesche* at Antwerp, thus helping to carry the Italian style to northern Europe, and much later in life, added a second of *Villanelle, moresche ed altre canzoni* (1581), also published in the north, at Paris. In all this music Lassus shuns any resemblance to the serious madrigal and keeps to a language of homophony and root-position chords, laid out in simple repetitive formal

Example 46

Lassus, 'O occhi manza mia'

[In your dear mind, my love, keep a thought for me, and give happiness]

schemes such as AABCC or AABBCC. His humour is often tinged with pathos, as in this last strain of *O occhi manza mia*, with its false relation (Example 46). To say that his *villanelle* sound almost hymn-like at times is not to liken them to church music, but rather to stress their simplicity of utterance. When we remember that he could be equally eloquent in writing French chansons, we can see where this simple tuneful style comes from; he was indeed the most cosmopolitan figure to turn his hand to the popular Italian secular forms. His sense of humour enabled him to poke fun at various nationalities. In his famous *Matona mia cara* he burlesques a German soldier serenading in Italian with an appalling accent ('matona' is how he would have pronounced

T.M.—D

'madonna'). Mimickry of a German accent classes this piece as a *tedesca*, just as the *moresca* provided a humourous dig at Negro slaves.

In the south there were composers such as Pomponio Nenna who still wrote the rustic type of three-part *villanella* with conspicuous fifths, and others who kept to the four-part medium, such as Filippo Azzaiolo. His *L'amanza mia*, with its clipped rhythmic patterns, represents the strumming of a mandoline to serenade a lady, while *Quando le sera* is a song about the cricket, the bird who sings through the hottest part of the day—an allegory of the ever-ardent suitor. This is a *villotta*, as evidenced by its dance-like alternations of '3/4' and '6/8' time.

Example 47
Marenzio, 'Io son amore'
[With bow and arrows I bait my trap]

Surprisingly, the three-part *villanella* found a follower in Marenzio, who published no fewer than five volumes of them between 1584 and 1587, all of which received several reprintings. Surprising, that is, in view of the normality of four parts and the preference one can all too easily imagine that Marenzio had for a texture which would allow plenty of contrast. In fact these works have all the polish and delicacy of his madrigals, and even though a few fifths are sprinkled around for regional colour there is nothing coarse about them. The close harmony of earlier years has given way to an airy SAB layout, as found in *Io son amore*, which more than ever suggests two upper voices with a continuo rather than a vocal bass—hints of the *concertato* duet. In Example 47 we see a sequence phrase which represents at once a transformation of the crude succession of triads with their fifths and an anticipation of something that was to become characteristic of later madrigalists, especially Monteverdi.

It is interesting that Marenzio's second volume of *villanelle* was actually entitled *Canzonette alla Napoletana*. Although the terms were sometimes synonymous, especially since *villanella* was an abbreviation for *canzon villanesca*, by the 1580s the *canzonetta* could also describe a genre whose style was rapidly approaching that of the light madrigal and which differed from it only through its strophic form. The wheel turned full circle: the madrigal, having started from the frottola, soon lost itself in the clouds but eventually descended again to the fields and woods of the light pastoral pieces, while the *villanella*, also related to the frottola, reached a new low in its bawdiness and nonsense language, only to be purified back by the efforts of proper madrigalists to the respectable, fifthless world of the 'new' *canzonetta*, as Einstein called it. Wert's *Canzonette villanelle* of 1589 are, as we might expect of such an intensely serious madrigalist, very little different from his madrigals—sophisticated versions of tunes from a popular native idiom. The fact that they are in five parts emphasizes this similarity, and the syllabic declamation and moments of brilliant counterpoint are entirely characteristic of Wert. Slightly more distinct in style are the light pieces of one or two figures who were known for these alone, such as Giuseppe Caimo, whose delightfully onomatopacic *canzonetta* about the cuckoo, *Mentre il cuculo*, is reprinted by Einstein, and Giovanni Ferretti, who had been publishing *Canzoni alla Napoletana* in five or even six parts since the 1560s. *Del crud'amor*, which Einstein also reprints, is an excellent example of a type which combines madrigalian seriousness and variety of texture with the playful rhythms of the *villanella* style.

In contrast to the assured competence of Ferretti's work stands a collection of Monteverdi's student compositions, the *Canzonette à 3* of 1584. Written at Cremona, this was the young composer's first published secular music, complimenting the *Sacrae Cantiunculae* of 1582, which are also in three parts. It shows great promise, as Monteverdi's teacher Ingegneri must have seen, though it looks as if both master and pupil regarded the three-part medium as a means of proving contrapuntal dexterity as well as one to delight polite society, for the pieces are full of studious imitations and ingenious interplay.

In the work of Orazio Vecchi both *canzonetta* and madrigal stand side by side in importance and in the artistry he brought to each. This is best seen in the large composite publication *Selva di varia ricreatione*, which appeared in 1590 and contained something for all social occasions, scored for from three to ten parts. Here even the *villotta* had lost its street connections and could be scored for six voices, as in *O bella, o bianca più*, though this does preserve its original dance-like rhythm. Some of these dance-like pieces were actually intended to accompany the dance, particularly the *balletto*, as its name implies. In this connection an important name is that of Giovanni Gastoldi, probably Wert's assistant at the Mantuan court. His *balletti* of 1595 are utterly simple five-part homophony in simple *villanella*-type shapes (e.g. AABCC), gay in rhythm but undistinguished otherwise, having *fa-las* at the end of the first and last lines. This music was more important historically than aesthetically, for it prompted the English vogue for the ballett, and also displayed a completely simplified approach to modern tonality which, as Kerman observes,[3] falls between the two stools of exploiting modal colouring and of actually planning the cadence schemes.

Right through the period of the folk-like *villanella* there existed a related sacred form, the *lauda*. Just as the *mascherate* discussed earlier were intended for staged entertainments, certain types of *lauda* provided music for the sacred plays that took the place of these during Lent; since both were directed at ordinary people, the musical style was much the same. This parallel is mentioned here to emphasize that there was no necessary distinction between sacred and profane in the Renaissance, and it is equally logical that, while the frottola and early Neapolitan *villanella* had their religious equivalent in the *lauda*, the later serious madrigal could be encountered in the guise of the *madrigale spirituale*. This form was the product of the Counter-Reformation and the resurgence of fervency inspired by the Jesuit movement, whose efforts were aimed at all classes of men. With their vernacular texts, spiritual madrigals were suitable in the context of court life for accompanying a prince or duke at his evening prayers, or in a social one for use by private groups or cultural academies during Lent, and perhaps on Sundays. In Rome, centre of the Papal court, they were especially popular, for naturally the amorous texts of secular madrigals were supposed to be anathema to the cardinals. Thus it is that Palestrina published two volumes of spiritual madrigals in five parts, in 1581 and 1594 respectively, while Marenzio wrote a volume of them which, significantly enough, appeared at Rome rather than Venice. Both men contributed to the flourishing market in anthologies of such pieces, carrying Jesuitical titles like *Diletto spirituale* or *Musicale essercitio*.

It must be said that this separate discussion of the spiritual madrigal is intended merely to highlight a genre which differed from the ordinary madrigal only in the circumstances of its use, not in its musical style, which never approached that of the motet. The textual boundary is a slender one, too, for certain Petrarch texts such as *I'vo piangendo*, settings of which have been mentioned elsewhere, were themselves quite suitable for, say, Good Friday meditation. A further instance of these delicate distinctions is found in *Qual mormorio soave*, from Marenzio's spiritual volume of 1584, which is pastoral in feeling: 'That sweet whispering of the breeze between the leafy branches'—but with Virgin rather than mistress at the centre of the tableau. All the typical devices of word painting abound—fast quavers for 'air and wind', slow, low chords for 'making silence', an element of the dialogue style when Marenzio places the Virgin's words with the three upper voices. Compositions like this are the musical equivalent of the many late Renaissance frescoes that adorn Roman churches, with their fervent spirit and lifelike atmosphere. Yet there is also a seriousness about them which is new in Marenzio's work and looks forward to his later, 'mannerist' period.

The spiritual madrigal flourished in northern Italy as well: one of many collections to appear at Venice was *Musica spirituale da diversi eccellentisimi musici* (1586), which contained Giovanni Gabrieli's only two works of this type. The texts were of higher quality than those of his secular madrigals and the music certainly matches anything in his madrigal output. The language is restrained but declamatory, as in the more progressive of his motets, and both pieces are laid out in a simple ABB form, in which the joins are cleverly concealed. In *Signor le tue man sante* the A section gradually builds up to a repeated exclamation 'O creator of heaven'; then follows this remarkably agitated climax, from which the music regains the central G minor through exquisite extra-modal modulations (Example 48). The B section begins on the word 'rinova'; its repeat after one statement is much less dramatic without the opening of Example 48, so that in both cases these joins are neatly dovetailed. Gabrieli adopts the opposite procedure in *Vergine il cui figliol*, in which the B section, opening with a full E♭ chord, first comes after a mild cadence of the upper voices on a unison G (G minor is again the 'home key'), and later follows much more dramatically upon a full G major chord without any break—a typically Gabrielian juxtaposition of unrelated keys.

Other spiritual madrigals to appear at Venice included five volumes by Philipp de Monte, a Franco-Fleming like Lassus who spent only

Example 48

G. Gabrieli, 'Signor le tue man sante'
[Already hidden in a mortal veil,
Renew your pious work]

part of his life in Italy. In fact the contrast in their temperaments can be seen in the fact that while Lassus wrote *villanelle* with as much facility as any other secular type of music, Monte shunned such levity, his less frivolous turn of mind being more appropriate for spiritual madrigals. His six-part setting of *Vergine pura* is a good example: strangely conservative in its modality and fickleness of harmony, it also displays some mannerist tendencies in distorting conventional textural and harmonic processes. Twice Monte juxtaposes D and B♭ major chords in mid-phrase, placing a strong verbal accent on the second of the two to add to the surprising effect. Although his rhythms are in *note nere*, moving by crotchets for the most part, there is an impressive and appropriate slowing down for 'i miei giorni tristi' as the poet pleads to the Virgin for consolation (Example 49). Notice

Example 49
Monte, 'Vergine pura'
[That my days of sadness
May be turned to joy]

how the unexpected pedal G emerges in the middle parts, supporting a curiously treated 6/4 chord, and the way Monte abruptly 'returns to joy'—and fast crotchets—in bar 41. Lassus turned to the spiritual madrigal at the end of his life. His very last work, the *Lagrime di San Pietro*, is a setting of a cycle of poems by Luigi Tansillo, set in austere seven-part counterpoint. It is symbolic of an increasingly gloomy religious outlook that beset him later in life.

The practice of writing spiritual madrigals declined after 1600; the madrigal was already changing in style and social function, and the place of the spiritual pieces was taken more and more by non-liturgical settings of Latin texts, particularly those in the new *concertato* style for a few voices and keyboard or lute continuo, which were intended for use in both church and 'princely apartment' as title-pages of collections proclaimed. Another fashion, which was not by any means new, was to substitute sacred words in Italian or Latin for original secular texts. A friend of Monteverdi's, Aquilino Coppini, turned many of his most famous early madrigals into suitable spiritual fodder for the Milanese, who being under reactionary Spanish domination were no doubt expected to prefer this to the profanities of amorous texts. It is perhaps for this reason that one hears of few native Milanese madrigalists.

1. op. cit., i, p. 373.

2. These are represented in L. Torchi, *L'Arte Musicale in Italia,* i (Milan, 1897), pp. 127 ff.

3. J. Kerman, *The Elizabethan Madrigal* (New York, 1962), p. 143.

7

THE MADRIGAL NORTH OF THE ALPS

In the discussion of the madrigal proper two great names have so far been conspicuous by their absence, namely Lassus and Monte, whom Einstein grouped with Wert as the 'three *oltremontani*'. But, as has been hinted from time to time, these two figures deserve to be distinguished from Wert in that only the earlier part of their lives was spent in Italy, and that by their more cosmopolitan character as composers and their returning to hold important musical positions north of the Alps they did more to 'internationalize' the madrigal and carry its influence outwards from Italy. Hence a chapter devoted to their work and that of later figures from the north who came under the Italian spell, and an attempt to take a comparative north-and-south view of the late sixteenth-century madrigal in Europe.

To this end we must review the changing position of Franco-Flemish composers in the late Renaissance. Whereas these men dominated Italian musical life at the time of the early madrigal (the more so in sacred music), and had been responsible for ennobling the frottola into the serious madrigal, by the 1560s there was a shift of the leadership into the hands of native Italians in both secular and sacred fields so that northerners no longer occupied the best positions. Yet Italy still exercised a fascination for them, as for all to whom the purpose of travel is to become cultured, and they still came south, as Lassus and Monte did at an impressionable age; for them the best positions were back over the Alps at the seats of the Imperial and Bavarian Courts. Now it was the Italians, led by the standard-bearer Andrea Gabrieli, who perfected and transformed the madrigal into something Italianate and more widely sociable, which was in its turn to attract the transalpines (in this case the English too) and dominate their efforts even more than the Franco-Flemings had dominated the earliest madrigal activity. For at least the latter set Italian texts by great poets, they did not import their native French chanson into Italy; the later madrigal, on the other hand, was exported all over Europe by being printed in all the big music-publishing centres—Antwerp, Paris, Munich, Leiden, Nuremberg. Most of Lassus's madrigals were published north of the Alps, though some later northerners did publish theirs at Venice, still the hub of madrigal-printing.

Lassus was born probably in 1532 at Mons, where he soon served as a choirboy. If it were not that he was kidnapped on account of his excellent voice he might never have gone to Italy, but as it was he was pressed into the Viceroy of Sicily's service at the age of twelve. During his ten years in Italy (1544–54) he was able to visit other Spanish dependencies such as Milan and Naples, and later became choirmaster at St John Lateran, Rome, just before Palestrina took over the post. A short stay in Antwerp, to supervise his first mixed publication of sacred and secular music in 1555, preceded his calling as a singer to Duke Albrecht V's court at Munich in 1556, and it was here he spent the rest of his life, becoming *Kapellmeister* a few years later. Though he did not travel much, we hear of one journey in 1562 with Andrea Gabrieli, to Bavaria, Bohemia and the Rhineland. He died in 1594.

By artistic training, he was an Italian, and his most significant contribution to that uniquely Italian genre, the madrigal, dates from his earlier years, when he was still full of the impressions his stay had left upon him. It was to Rore, not the earlier madrigalists, that he was most indebted, particularly in connection with his early chromatic experiments: his Latin ode *Alma nemes* was modelled on Rore's celebrated one *Calami sonum ferentes*, and he espoused the chromatic cause with vigour in the weird progressions of the *Prophetiae Sybillarum*. Later on these intense modulations became part and parcel of his sacred style, which came to breathe the fervent spirit of the Counter Reformation, while in madrigals he became less extreme and was happy to rely on existing formulas.[1] In his choice of texts, however, he remained aware of new possibilities: he set much of Tasso and Guarini, and found that words with a religious undertone matched the mood of melancholy which, as we have seen, seemed to descend over him in later years.

Einstein imputes to Lassus's madrigals a 'conciseness and impatience' of style,[2] and it is certainly true that, compared with Rore, he preferred the short phrase. One can already see this in the brusque interruption 'così sempre facciamo' (and so we always do) set in jerky rhythms during the otherwise sad course of the early *Occhi piangete* (1555), and in a much later piece, *Come la notte* (*c.* 1583), the more even alternations of slow minim and fast crotchet movement succeed one another quite quickly. Conciseness, reflected in largely syllabic word-setting, is a particular feature of the later madrigals, some of which are largely chordal in the manner of the *villanella*. In contrapuntal treatment, too, Lassus is similarly economical, using double ideas sounded together to bring in the voices as quickly as is compatible with independent part-writing. Whether in four or (most frequently) in five parts, Lassus often thinks vertically, his bass line being full of leaps and providing the harmonic foundation to melodies which may also be quite angular in contour.

His approach to word-setting is marked by restraint. Despite what he learned in other respects from Rore, he did not seem so concerned with affective underscoring of emotional meanings, and later on his madrigals thrived on more than mere delicate musical imagery of the kind that the new generation of Italians were writing. Typical of this spirit is the opening of his early *Crudele acerba* (Book I à 5, 1555), with its subtle use of suspension: notice how the voices sink in pitch down to the word 'morte' (Example 50). In case it may be thought that not enough distinction has been made between the 'seriousness' of the Rore generation and the later 'seriousness' of the mannerists which came as a reaction to a surfeit of Arcadian delights, compare this opening and Wert's on the same text, quoted in Example 38 in Chapter 5, to see the tremendous difference. Lassus can adopt conventional modes of word-painting, it is true (the run of quavers for 'fugge' in *Come la notte*, for instance), but later in life he prefers other means of infusing an intimate personal feeling into his music; he is better at creating an overall mood than in highlighting individual phrases of text in the manner of Rore or Marenzio. The four-part *Spesso in poveri alberghi*, from another of his mixed collections published in 1573 and dedicated to the Fugger brothers in Augsburg, is a fine example of his personal style—a setting of a text from Ariosto's *Orlando Furioso* which is an attack on the unfriendliness found in courtly palaces. It is full of uneasy harmonic changes, distant flatwards modulations, and jarring syncopations, and even has an archaic triple suspension (bar 5). It is easy to see from Example 51 how the 'flat' extra-modal harmonies arise quite naturally through *musica ficta*, but

Example 50
Lassus, 'Crudele acerba'
[Cruel, bitter, inexorable death]

since this is the ending, we can be sure that Lassus intended the final plagal cadence to sound unsettled and inconclusive. Even the bland 6/3 triads, such a useful standby in his chordal settings of church music, create tension by their repetitive rhythms.

It is through this kind of exploitation of harmony and decaying modality that Lassus creates the intense moods of his madrigals and shows a subtle feeling for the texts he sets. He does not rely much on dissonance, but prefers to surprise the listener by an unexpected harmonic turn. An especially common one is the V–IV 'interrupted' cadence, which occurs twice during this very beautiful conclusion of the setting of *Cantai, or piango* (1555). The 'bitterness' is also captured in the unusual dissonance* (Example 52). Another equally exquisite

Example 51
Lassus, 'Spesso in poveri alberghi'
[Nor does one see a friendship that is not false]

ending is that of *Occhi piangete*, with its spacious treatment of a sequential phrase 'lamentar piu'.

Whereas Lassus's madrigals were but a fraction of his whole output, Philipp de Monte (1521–1603) could be described as a compulsive composer of madrigals, with an output of well over 1,000 to his credit. These appeared in one volume *à 3*, four volumes *à 4*, nineteen *à 5*, and eight *à 6*, and this not counting the odd publication of spiritual pieces. Monte was born at Malines and became a friend of Lassus when he was a singer in the chapel of Philip II of Spain at Naples in the 1550s; he also visited England around this time, but much of his later life was spent in the employment of the Imperial Court at Vienna and then Prague, where he died. He might have had even more contact with Lassus had he achieved the post at Munich for which the Chancellor at Brussels recommended him in 1555, but as it was they often worked together on assignments, well earning Einstein's description 'musical twins'. Monte was less versatile than Lassus, and more inclined to gravity, for he wrote no *villanelle* despite his stay in Naples. Einstein distinguishes three periods in his prodigiously productive career: his Italian period, his middle 'crisis of style' period and a final resolution in a backward-looking manner, unable to come to terms

Example 52
Lassus, 'Cantai, or piango'
[So sweet, and the root of my bitterness]

with the wittiness of Marenzio and his followers, as he himself admitted
in the dedication of his Book VIII *à 5* (1580):

Imperial Majesty . . . we see that up to now everyone is doing his best to lead
music to great perfection by means of a new style . . . I have done all I could
to find a way to give more pleasure to those who should and can form a
judgement on it, but it is perhaps true that the more I try the less I succeed . . .[3]

In fact he later acknowledged modern trends by using the more
'concerto-like' texture of divided sopranos and building the texture
from briefer musical motives.

Monte's earlier style shows the influence of Willaert in the full,
closely woven texture, the long-breathed paragraphs, and the careful
declamation of words, all well exemplified in a five-part elegy for low

Example 53
Monte, 'Verament'in amore'
[But this is all that is left him:
Rapture for one short hour, then the end
Of all his delight]

voices (*Carlo ch'en tenerella acerba etade*) published in his Book II *à* 5
(1567). Completely contrasted is the dainty five-part *Verament'in amore*
(Book V, 1574), a 'hit' of Monte's middle period. Here the middle lines
of this brief *sestet* are set chordally with delightful rhythms, and a
strong feeling of tonality pervades the whole, whether in the F♯s,
E♭s and B♮s of the opening or the playful alternations of B♭ and
G minor later on. It is not hard to see why this madrigal remained
popular through reprintings right up to 1614. Here is part of the
chordal passage (Example 53), given to the upper four voices and later
taken up with varied harmonies by the tutti.

   This rhythmic liveliness persisted in Monte's later madrigals,
accompanied by a precise but fragmentary treatment of musical
material. That this approach was particularly successful when writing
for a big ensemble of seven parts can be seen from his setting of
Boccaccio's text *Già fu chi m'hebbe cara*, published in 1599. Although
conventional enough by comparison with what was being written
by the younger generation, this *canzona* in four stanzas possesses a
grandeur not often encountered in the emotional outpourings of the

mannerists. Monte's concern for formal articulation is apparent in each verse, for the first and third are laid out in ABB, and the second and fourth more subtly in ABC'BC″C″—a more complex scheme involving variation. As if this were not enough, the text has a refrain at the end of stanzas 2 and 4, so that all but the A section in these verses is heard twice, giving an overall coherence to the four stanzas as a whole. As for the sound of the music, it is immensely varied in colour and by no means lacking in warm, impassioned moments. In particular, the C″ section from stanzas 2 and 4, heard four times in all, is worth a close aural investigation. What a splendid dissonance occurs at the asterisk (Example 54)! It breaks all the rules and has the theorists, even the editors, tut-tutting (Einstein puts an exclamation mark by the soprano's middle C); it is caused by the complete independence of tenor II, with his conventional 'sigh' suspension and the rigid soprano imitation, which in turn brings about the pathetic minor sixth that follows immediately—and again when tenor II picks up the same figure. The imitations have been bracketed and the bass figured to make this clear. The somewhat static bass line helps to weld the whole texture together.

Lassus and Monte were figures of international repute who came to Italy and became involved with the madrigal because when they were young men there were still posts for northerners, especially through political connections between Spain (who held sway in many parts of Italy) and the Low Countries. In any case the would-be cultured musician could ill afford not to go there to sample Renaissance life to the full. But later men from the north went to Italy with a different aim: not to fill posts, which were now occupied by Italians, but to learn from these same Italians and to diffuse the fruits of their learning back over the Alps—a process that was to ensure the hegemony of the Italian manner during so much of the Baroque era. German song was quickly engulfed by a tide of Italian influence from the year 1566 onwards; this date marked the first publication in Germany of settings of Italian texts, Antonio Scandello's first book of *Canzone Napoletane*. The first important German to go and study in Italy was Hans Leo Hassler (1564–1612), who worked under Andrea Gabrieli in the 1580s and became a lifelong friend of Giovanni. His later posts were with the Fugger family at Augsburg (also patrons of the Gabrielis), at Nuremberg and with the Elector of Saxony. His German *Lieder* are a happy mixture of German and Italian qualities, but it is the two

Example 54

Monte, 'Già fu chi m'hebbe cara'

[That in a vain, weary sigh, sweetheart]

publications with Italian texts that concern us here, for it is in these
that his grasp of the Italianate vein can best be assessed. Both appeared
at Augsburg, one of Germany's important music-printing centres,
during Hassler's time there. The *Canzonetta à 4* of 1590 show that he
knew all there was to know about the 'new' *canzonette* as exemplified
not in the works of his teacher but those of Vecchi, with its lightweight,
facile counterpoint and dainty homophonic strains. This was just the
sort of jolly, entertaining music that found favour in England too:
it seemed to travel better than the more serious Italian style. The very
first number in the collection, *Ridon di maggio*, has a typical sectional
form AABCC with dance-like triple time for C, and some sequential
writing (rather like Example 47 of Chapter 6) in B. A more contrapuntal approach is found in *Io son ferito*, based on a theme by Palestrina
that was very popular among composers of lighter music. Interesting
here is the twofold setting of the last line, once in black notes and
once in white, with a long coda over a tenor pedal; since the words
in each verse speak of death, grief, or wounds, the music happens to
fit well each time.

In the *Madrigali à 5, 6, 7 & 8 voci* of 1596 Hassler shows himself to be
a kind of Teutonic Marenzio, though his style is never quite as deft
as the Italian's; he is fond of cliché progressions like G major–A minor–
E major and of artificial devices like sequence, which he might have
picked up from Monteverdi's earliest madrigals. If one heard *Ardo, si*
one would guess early Marenzio, but the phrases are a little too short,
the cadences too predictable, though the suspensions at 'perfida e
dispietata' bring hope of better things; certainly the *seconda parte*,
with text by Tasso (the first is Guarini), receives a more sympathetic
setting, with some fine sequences towards the end (Example 55). For
a more specifically Venetian influence we must look to the double-
choir madrigals in this collection, one of which thrives on echo effects
in a rather trite way. The best is *Al merto et al valore*, whose opening
is quoted in Example 56. Notice how Hassler tosses the fanfare-like
'Verona applaude' figure against the entry of choir II. His command
of sonority in the tuttis is impressive, too. This Venetian manner also
strongly affected Hassler's double-choir German *Lieder*.

Hassler studied with Andrea Gabrieli; many others came to Venice
to learn from Giovanni. Venice itself exerted a powerful attraction
to those from over the Alps, as to anyone who undertook the 'grand
tour'. Geographically it was the closest city to the Imperial Lands and

Example 55
Hassler, 'Ardo, si'
[Let the disdain of your foolish heart be thwarted]

Germany, and it was famous all over Europe for its rich and progressive
culture. Couple these factors with the Gabrieli family's reputation and
connections, and one can see why it was to Venice rather than Rome
or Milan that the northerners went. If Hassler had only to cross the
Alps from Bavaria, others came from further afield: Johann Grabbe
from Westphalia, Mogens Pedersøn and Hans Nielsen from the
Danish court of King Christian IV. These men are singled out since
they published madrigals during the years 1606–9 which were the
fruit of their studies; nine of these have fortunately been reprinted[4]
and show us exactly what they must have learned in Italy. They are
written in an almost *concertato* style: that is, the independent vocal
writing is underpinned by a basic harmonic framework that could
be realized by a continuo, though this is not specified, and the vocal
texture is always complete in itself. Vividness of contrast is the hallmark
—especially between long notes in lower voices, like pedals, and short
snatches of canon or interweaving thirds above them; Baroque
expressionism is already present in impassioned melodic intervals like
the minor sixth and diminished fourth, in the abrupt, dramatic silences,
in the augmented triads and juxtapositions of unrelated chords, the

Example 56
Hassler, 'Al merto et al valore'
[Verona, applaud merit and courage]

bold word-painting and chromaticism, and in the tendency towards
a brilliantly ornamental melody. Gabrieli knew how to impart to these
young men an ability to control the emotional rise and fall in a madrigal, as we can see in this remarkable moment from Grabbe's *Lasso*,

Example 57
Grabbe, 'Lasso, perché mi fuggi'
[If you have so much desire for my death,
 Why, alas, do you flee me?]

perché mi fuggi (Example 57). An intense *crescendo* seems almost written
into the vocal scoring in this piling up of short motives. Nothing could
be more violently contrasted than the simultaneous use of breve and
semi-quaver at 'lasso'.

It is tempting to assume that these pupils must have modelled their
madrigals on Giovanni Gabrieli's motets, particularly the most

'Baroque' ones of his late years, rather than on his madrigals, which seem to show no hint of this highly intense, modern manner; tempting, until we remember that no Gabrieli madrigals have survived from after 1595, and that the remaining seventeen years of his life were crucial to his style as well as to the evolution of the Baroque in general. That he must have written madrigals in the new manner we can be sure, on the evidence of madrigal-like motets such as the wild *Timor et tremor*. If so, this would explain the almost Monteverdian boldness of his pupils' work (no doubt both he and they were aware of what Monteverdi was up to in his Books IV and V). The only respect in which their work was not fully up-to-date was in the lack of a continuo, but this was for the very good reason that Gabrieli insisted on their mastering strict five-part counterpoint in which the vocal texture was complete and required no easy 'filling in': this is what 'strict' meant to Gabrieli—there was no strait jacket of rules and regulations of the kind normally implied more recently by that forbidding term 'strict counterpoint', so many of which are but figments of theorists' imaginations when it comes to living music. Apart from the ban on a continuo Gabrieli allowed his pupils freedom of imagination.

The one who revelled in this freedom more than anybody was the brilliant young German, Heinrich Schütz, whom Gabrieli taught during the last years of his life (1609–12). Schütz was 24 when he arrived in Venice; within two years he published his opus 1, a volume of five-part madrigals. The Baroque features are even more marked in these youthful and exuberant pieces than in the earlier pupils' work, and one might almost say that they were at times too extravagant, something readily forgiven in the efforts of an apprentice. Take *Fuggi o mio core*, for instance—Schütz clearly revels in the opening trumpetings, the vocal contortions at 'ferire' (wound) in bars 19–20, and the agonized build-up to a dominant seventh in bar 24. The words are set syllabically to the clipped phrases of the *concertato* manner. In general Schütz prefers (no doubt on Gabrieli's instigation) to manipulate the five voices rather than to play off contrasted smaller groups. Among the many bold expressive devices chromaticism does not loom large, and it seems unlikely that Gesualdo's madrigals would have appealed to him. Monteverdi's must have done, for the dramatic utterance of *Dunque addio*, with its choral declamation, telling silences and sighing rests, strongly recall the Mantuan's style. By way of quotation, here is one of Schütz's most exuberant moments of contrast,

Example 58

Schütz, 'Ride la primavera'

[Alas, you have encased your heart with eternal ice]

from *Ride la primavera*, a spring song. The music describes by its chilling harmonies the 'eternal ice that has gripped the heart'—referring metaphorically to Cloris' refusal to thaw out to her lover (Example 58). This is not the neurotic contrast between brilliant *agitato* and slow chromatics beloved of Gesualdo, but something more controlled and no less expressive. These madrigals were an auspicious beginning for Schütz, who was now excellently placed to disseminate all he had learned of the *stile nuovo* back in his native Germany.

1. Einstein, op. cit., ii, p. 486.
2. ibid., ii, p. 486.
3. Quoted ibid., ii, p. 510.
4. *Das Chorwerk*, xxxv (Wolfenbüttel, 1935).

8

THE MADRIGAL IN ENGLAND

In the development of the English madrigal we have the most fascinating non-Italian offshoot of the central madrigal tradition. Despite
England's strong native culture there arose in the last years of the
sixteenth century a pronounced vogue for things Italian which was
reflected not only in musical but also in poetic taste (the Arcadian
movement in English poetry led by Sir Philip Sidney). The Channel
was in no way a symbol of English isolation in the Elizabethan period,
and Italian culture not only exerted a powerful attraction on the
artistically-minded Englishman, it provided a guiding light and an
inspiration for scholars. Aspects of Italian Renaissance court life
tickled the English fancy: Castiglione's *Il Cortegiano* (*The Courtier*),
published in Italy in 1528 and mentioning the importance of music
as a courtly accomplishment, was translated by Sir Thomas Hoby in
1561.[1] Italian musicians were employed at the English court, even
though this was not generally the way through which Italian music—
particularly madrigals—reached English circles, and there was also
the grand tour for men of leisure or of letters, whereby Italian taste
could be savoured at first hand.

But few composers were among those able to benefit from the grand
tour, or at least the visit to Venice which formed so exciting a part of
it; indeed English composers did not usually enjoy the opportunities
for travel that brought Continental non-Italians like Hassler into
direct contact with Italian madrigalists. This may well be why the
English madrigal got under way so late, nearly sixty years after its
Italian model and well after other symptoms of the Italianization of
English culture were noticeable. On the other hand it would be an

over-simplification to regard Nicholas Yonge's anthology of Italian madrigals with English texts, *Musica Transalpina* (1588), as the very inception of the new trend. To go into print there has to be a growing demand of some years' standing, and Yonge himself explains the nature of that demand in his preface:

Since I first began to keepe house in this Citie, it hath been no small comfort unto mee, that a great number of Gentlemen and Merchants of good accompt (as well of this realm as of forreine nations) have taken in good part such entertainment of pleasure, as my poor abilitie was able to affoord them, both by the exercise of Musicke daily used in my house, and by furnishing them with Bookes of that kinde yeerely sente me out of Italy and other places, which beeing for the most part Italian Songs, are for sweetnes of Aire, verie well liked of all, but most in account with them that understand that language.[2]

Yonge was a collector of the latest Italian madrigal publications supplied by travelling merchants, in much the same way as today's connoisseur collects the latest trends in Scandinavian design, and his house was, as it were, a 'madrigal centre'. He was also a professional musician, being a lay-clerk of St Paul's Cathedral, so that it would be untrue to describe his singing sessions as amateur activity, or to conclude from his preface that men in all walks of English life were gifted amateur musicians. These, as Woodfill is at pains to point out,[3] were largely confined to the higher and wealthier reaches of society, and the popularity of the madrigal was not simply the result of the innate musicianship of English society as a whole. In fact, though by comparison with the new professionalism in Italy the English madrigal was aimed at amateur groups, these could resemble the cultural gatherings of the Italian academies in their social composition; it was just that their aim lay in the realm of musical enjoyment rather than æsthetic pursuits of a more academic nature.

Indeed, the wider interests of the Italian academies were not reflected among England's madrigal fanciers because they did not expect madrigal-singing to be a poetic as well as a musical experience. There was no fund of poetry exactly comparable to that of Petrarch, Ariosto or Tasso, that would have been suitable for composers to set had they been at all interested in the literary aspect of madrigal composition—which they were not, for even the Italianate poetry of Sidney was rarely set to music: composers preferred either translated forms of Italian verse, or texts which in form and spirit were modelled for the purpose of being set to music on certain Italian types. Such texts had a freshness and a lesser degree of elegance and sophistication than their Italian counterparts. The English composers avoided long, cyclic poems in many verses as too 'poetic' a challenge, unsuited to their ideas of musical structure. Yonge's translations of Italian madrigals immediately provided a quarry of suitable texts, to which was shortly added those in Thomas Watson's *Italian Madrigals Englished* in 1590 which, though it undoubtedly spurred on interest in Italian madrigalian poets, presented translations of their poems that showed scant respect for their qualities. For the rest, English madrigal verse remained, if not actually translated, Italianate in feeling and lightweight in tone; it was never related to a literary movement in the way that Italian madrigal poetry had always been.

What of the musical attributes of *Musica Transalpina*? The greater part of its contents were five-part pieces, as might be expected, but there were a fair number of four-part and a few six-part ones. The mixture of composers represented, progressive and conservative styles, new and not so new pieces, and madrigal and canzonet forms, emphasizes the impression of current confusion in the development of the Italian madrigal, which was also to some extent responsible for the problematic nature of the English development. For example, while the 1580s saw the *rapprochement* of the new *canzonetta* and the light madrigal in Italy, in England the distinctions were imperfectly understood, as can be seen from the confused nomenclature on title-pages when compared with the music they were supposed to entitle, and the result was to be found in confusing mergers of forms and types— ballett and canzonet, canzonet and light madrigal, and so on. Yonge's choice of composers is interesting. Marenzio figures largely in the five-part selection with works from his Book I *à* 5, but there are even more by Alfonso Ferrabosco, whose importance should not be overlooked, since he was the one Italian composer who migrated to England and whose madrigals had been circulating in manuscript copies as well as more recently printed ones. For four-part pieces Yonge favours Palestrina, which is not surprising when we remember that he was the only notable Italian who still preferred this texture for serious madrigals: Yonge chooses from his recent Book II of 1586. For six-part works Marenzio and Ferrabosco again dominate. Canzonets are represented in works by Ferretti and others, though their small number is out of proportion to their later significance in England.

Then there are a number of Flemish compositions which suggest that Yonge knew well the Flemish anthologies published by Phalèse in Antwerp; certainly the gathering together of madrigals for different scorings in one volume, later so characteristic of the English madrigal, was a Flemish rather than an Italian habit of publishers.

Watson's *Italian Madrigals Englished* of 1590 constitutes a fervent piece of propaganda on behalf of one Italian composer: Marenzio. The tone is more serious because of this, though no extreme madrigals are chosen, and all the five-part ones are again drawn from his Book I. By contrast the later anthologies—the second *Musica Transalpina* and Morley's *Selected Canzonets* (both 1597) and his *Selected Madrigals* (1598) rapidly redress the balance towards the lighter-weight music of Marenzio, Vecchi and many other minor Italians, which seems more in accord with Morley's taste and that of the later English composers who followed the lead he gave.

The appearance of these Italian anthologies collected by Yonge, Watson and Morley, together with the circulation of Ferrabosco's work provided the complex network whereby the Italian madrigal style was transmitted to the later English composers. But it is important not to forget that the English also had a native tradition of secular song during the sixteenth century which continued to flourish alongside the madrigal and sometimes cross-fertilized with it. In his admirable book on the Elizabethan madrigal Kerman rightly sought to disentangle this quite separate indigenous development which had hitherto been lumped with the madrigal to the greater confusion of the history of both.[4] Without wishing to paraphrase his chapter on English song, it need only be said here that the presence of this tradition modified certain Italianate features of English madrigals. With its adherence to modal and 'folk-like' harmonic and melodic inflections, and its emphasis on the uppermost or 'singing' part, it lent a certain distinctive character, particularly to some of Wilbye's madrigals.

The two important composers who belong to the history of English song rather than to that of the madrigal are Byrd and Gibbons. In particular Byrd's *Psalms, Sonnets and Songs*, published contemporaneously with *Musica Transalpina* in 1588, belong to the genre of accompanied solo song, in which the top voice is the 'first singing part' and the others are played, though words are underlaid in such a way that they could be sung too. Unlike the strict and serious style of the psalms and songs, some of the 'pastorals' have a more popular flavour

and a more energetic counterpoint. The attractive *Though Amaryllis
dance* is a good example, conceived in a very free alternation of 6/4
and 3/2 with consequent flexibility of rhythm and frequent cross-
accents. But this is far removed from the madrigal style, which only
affected Byrd's writing in his second publication under a similar title
(1611). This contains a chromatic composition, *Come woeful Orpheus*,
inspired by, or perhaps intended as a parody of, madrigalian excesses;
and also the four-part version of *This sweet and merry month of May*, the
only genuinely Italianate madrigal Byrd ever wrote. The latter, since
it was originally included in four- and six-part settings in Watson's
anthology of 1590, also possesses the distinction of being the very first
published English madrigal, though for Byrd it no doubt represented a
passing gesture of acknowledgement to the new taste and nothing
more, for he never wrote anything else like it. Gibbons was not a
madrigalist either, in any sense of the word, despite his loose use of the
word madrigal in the title of his secular publication of 1612: the
ethical tone of some of his texts bears no resemblance to the madrigal
verse customarily set by the madrigalists, and Kerman has shown how
one piece, *What is our life?*, is really an adapted song in the style of the
verse anthem.[5]

Such were the developments in England that led to the madrigal
and those that stood apart from it. They should be compared with the
much more straightforward conditions whereby the Italian madrigal
tradition was transmitted to other countries abroad. In this connection
Arnold's remarks in a review of an edition of Danish madrigals in
1967 are appropriate:

One remains thankful for the English channel, and even more for our break
with Rome which made it rare for the Englishman to travel. Instead of studying
directly with the 'famed Italian masters', as the Danes could, they had to
acquire their knowledge of *Musica Transalpina* at second hand.[6]

The English madrigal was a rare example of the naturalization of a
foreign form. By this fact it distinguishes itself from French, German
or Spanish vernacular secular music, whose national characteristics
were always clearly differentiated and which continuously evolved
over a longer period despite a measure of Italian influence. This is
why a consideration of the madrigal as a whole must include the
English type while excluding the French chanson, the German *Lied*
or the Spanish *villancico*.

Perhaps it was the English character which gave the madrigal genre a greater objectivity of outlook and a stronger leaning towards purely musical invention than the native Italian type possessed. On the whole they preferred a grander design in single pieces, with a fuller musical working-out. The drama and passion of the Italians was alien to them, so that the extreme chromaticism (indeed, chromatics in general) and techniques of choral declamation typical of the mannerists were never to be found in their work. Their art was, in Einstein's words, nearer to nature and less exclusive in the sense that it was addressed not to patrons of one kind and another but to amateur groups. The freakish, intensive atmosphere of the development is seen in the fact that most madrigals were produced in the two decades from 1588 to 1608.

Even more concentrated than this were the activities of Thomas Morley (1557–1602), the man who more than all others determined the direction that English taste in madrigal-writing would take. Nearly all his publications date from the 1590s, and after 1601 he withdrew from the madrigal scene. Of all the English composers, he owed most to Italian influence; his art was the most derivative, providing a less diluted style for his followers to modify. This was partly because he was a theorist with a keen perceptiveness for foreign styles, and that he was well informed about the essence of the contemporary Italian madrigal we can see from his remarks about it in the *Plaine and Easie Introduction*. The paradox is that his actual compositions do not conform to this description. He is not a madrigalist so much as a writer of canzonets, a preference that shows a taste for lighter music entirely characteristic of the English madrigal as a whole. His fondness for the four-, three- or even two-part scorings is unrelated to the serious madrigal, for even though Marenzio did write such pieces à 4, they are more sophisticated than anything in the English development —in the same way that Beethoven's quartets differ from Mozart's smaller serenades. Their Italian models belong in the realm of the frivolous light madrigal and canzonet.

The unusual scoring of Morley's *Canzonets to Two Voices* (1595) may well have been connected with a didactic purpose. It was customary to use two-part music for instruction in singing or playing in the sixteenth century, just as these pieces have in more recent times provided material for teachers of counterpoint. But it is interesting that some are still based on Italian models: not two-part canzonets, which did not exist, but four-part ones, by people like Felice Anerio.

The three- and four-part scorings were altogether more popular among Morley's followers. The *Canzonets to Three Voices* (1593) were Morley's first publication; it is here that we first encounter confusing nomenclature, for these are actually madrigals rather than canzonets. The tone is mostly light, and though the lighter pieces have no pretentions—i.e. they are not miniature full-scale madrigals—neither are they always entirely frivolous in feeling, for Morley the theorist was if nothing else a good contrapuntist. Some of the pieces stand apart

Example 59
Morley, 'Deep lamenting'

in that they really are attempts at seriousness in both choice of text and musical idiom. It is curious that Morley should experiment in this way with a three-part texture, which hardly affords the scope for dissonant writing appropriate to a text that begins with the words *Deep lamenting*. But if it lacks pathos, the setting is still couched in an earnest contrapuntal style, and creates tension as best it can by rather old-fashioned methods. The falling thirds at the opening, for instance, are as old as Josquin's famous motet *Absalon fili mi*, written at the beginning of the century, when they must have sounded much more modern and daring. At times Morley's piece sounds like a watered-down four-part texture, especially the setting of 'now mayst thou laugh full merrily', where the middle voice seems to be doubling as tenor and also in a typical pair-alternation formula (Example 59), or at other moments of more heartfelt expression, when one's ear almost supplies an extra suspension that a fourth voice would have made possible (e.g. 'O no, weep not').

Like these canzonets, Morley's *Madrigals to Four Voices*, published in the following year (1594), also fall into two groups, light and serious, the lighter pieces again being more numerous. Among these are Morley's best narrative madrigals, and also the popular *April is in my mistress' face*, a delightful canzonet-like piece resembling though not parodying a work with a similar text by Vecchi. Here the canzonet element is seen in the hinted repeat of the opening line and the actual repeat of the final one. The entirely Italianate feeling is not to be found in all these light madrigals, however: *On a fair morning*, for example, though it is scored in the bright Italian manner for SAAB (the use of three upper voices is indicative of this), is in other respects distinctly English in flavour. The tonal ambivalence of the opening phrase, starting in F and ending in G, recalls the modality of folksong, and certain devices like changing notes and false relations are used in a particularly English way. The consistently jerky, bucolic rhythms and at times curious underlay stand in contrast to Italianate smoothness, too. The serious madrigals in the 1594 collection show Morley to be ill-at-ease with this type, as can be seen in *Die now, my heart*. This setting adopts the *alla breve* style with basic minim beat, and its counterpoint is somewhat dry and redolent of the academic tradition; in fact the words 'O think not, Death, alas thy dart will pain me' are set to a pair-alternation almost identical with a four-part version of Example 59. This approach, whose blandness shows scant respect for the words, could have strayed from a text-book demonstration of the device of alternating pairs. It is only at the final couplet 'O hear a doleful wretch's crying' that Morley rises to a new expressive level, using the slower rhythm of *alla breve* writing to prolong the tension of the dissonances.

The contents of the *Canzonets to Five and Six Voices* of 1597 are more closely related to Italian models by Ferretti and others, who had developed a tradition of 'monumental canzonet' (i.e. the five- and six-part type) over several decades. But whereas in the *Canzonets to Two Voices* Morley had simplified his models down to the most fragile of contrapuntal textures, in these he shows the more characteristic English trait of making a very simple basic style into something richer and more musically varied. This does not necessarily mean sacrificing the epigrammatic brevity of the Italian canzonet: *Cruel, with thou persever?* is only 36 bars long. But it nevertheless displays a contrapuntal ingenuity not found in the Italians' work. It is also unusual in repeating the second rather than the first section of the canzonet to make an ABBCC form, by restating the reply 'peace shalt thou have' to the question embodied in the opening lines.

Of all the Italian forms imported into England, none was as derivative as the ballett, and none proves more clearly in comparison that the English sought greater musical variety than the Italians were content with. In making this comparison between Morley's *Balletts to Five Voices* of 1595 and Gastoldi's *Balletti* of 1591, we must again distinguish —as so often in Morley's hybrid publications—between the simpler type of ballett based on Gastoldi's and those which are more like canzonets, with more contrapuntal interest, and even a modicum of word-painting. Perhaps Morley's most straightforward ballett is the famous *Now is the month of Maying*, not directly based on Gastoldi—its text is in fact borrowed from one used by Vecchi—but coming closest to the former's symmetrical homophonic style. Both halves, each of which is repeated, consist of balanced eight-bar phrases, four bars of verse and four of *fa-la*; only the second *fa-la* is in any way contrapuntal.

A comparison of a Morley ballett actually based on a Gastoldi model and the original model will point the more usual contrast between the English and Italian types. Morley's *Shoot false love I care not* has a text based upon Gastoldi's *Viver lieto voglio*, and both are in the G mode. Morley's more adventurous view of 'tonality' is evident in that he begins on a C major chord, giving an unusual slant to the modal feeling, and comes round to D major after four bars, creating a sense of tonal balance, after which the first *fa-la* strongly confirms G. In the much longer second half, his key-scheme is varied and purposeful: cadences occur on C, D (half-close), G, D, A minor, and D in the verse alone. Gastoldi's on the other hand is repetitive and lacking in direction: several C major cadences produced by overlapping groups of different voices, a D major one, then back to C again. When he regains G for the *fa-la*, it is without much sense of 'arrival' compared with Morley's circle-of-fifths approach. If the verses, then, show the two composers' attitudes to tonal possibilities, the treatment of the *fa-las* emphasizes other aspects of Morley's adventurousness. Gastoldi's first *fa-la* continues with the same duple beat as the verse, and its only concession to textural variety lies in the use of an answering effect between one voice and the other four (Example 60a). Morley's not only contains lively cross-rhythms but also contrasts of rhythmic pace within the texture. Whereas Gastoldi's bass merely acts as a harmonic support, Morley's is much more than that (Example 60b). Its conjunct

Example 60 (a)
Gastoldi, 'Viver lieto voglio'

nature is even more marked in Morley's second *fa-la*, where the bold falling scale bears a delicate contrapuntal fabric. Here Gastoldi simply reverts to the dialogue of his first *fa-la* with the melodic tag inverted. Morley extends his section to nine bars of polyphonic writing which makes a contrast with the previous homophony and a climax to the whole piece. In general Morley invests greater musical invention in the *fa-la* refrains of his balletts than in the verses, and his contrapuntal intricacy is something which Gastoldi never attempts. This is entirely

T.M.—E

characteristic of the English preference for musical working-out: Gastoldi's utterly simple rhythms, intended for dancing, lacked the interest needed to make singing for purely musical enjoyment worth while. This would account, too, for Morley's clearly thought-out cadence schemes, which compare with the 'drab and amorphous' effect of Gastoldi's, as Kerman observes.

Very few of Morley's works so far discussed are in fact madrigals. For an excellent example of one of these there is the six-part setting

Example 60 (b)
Morley, 'Shoot false love I care not'

of *Hard by a crystal fountain*, published in *The Triumphs of Oriana* (1601), an anthology in honour of Queen Elizabeth which sums up all the Italianate trends in the English madrigal of the 1590s. Even this brilliant work is a parody of an Italian model, Croce's *Ove tra l'herbe e i fiori*, itself published in *Il Trionfo di Dori* (1592), the Italian prototype for the English *Triumphs*. As with Gastoldi's *balletti*, Morley sets out to expand and develop an Italian piece whose style is simpler and comparatively featureless in character, by enlarging the key-range and the scope of the contrapuntal treatment, and adding many felicitous touches of word-painting.[7] Morley would have known Croce's piece through its appearance in Yonge's second *Musica Transalpina* in 1597.

A mention of this madrigal makes a fitting end to a consideration of the most Italianate of English madrigalists, who exerted such a formative influence upon other members of the school.

If Morley approached the madrigal mainly through the smaller three- and four-part textures, Thomas Weelkes (*c.* 1575–1623) showed a preference for larger combinations of voices and more panoramic designs. His *Balletts and Madrigals* of 1598 contain five-part balletts which in some cases further Morley's type as seen in the 1595 collection, and in others seem even more intricate and less Italianate in style. *To shorten winter's sadness* is one of the former, with a chordal verse and a contrapuntal *fa-la* with strong rhythmic contrasts. A more subtle design is present in *On the plains, fairy trains*, in which the verses are no longer simply chordal and rhythms are much more varied: snatches of triple time occur appropriately on the words 'now they dance, now they prance' and the whole of the second *fa-la* is written in this metre (Example 61). Yet another ballett, *Sing we at pleasure*, is in triple time throughout—not the homophonic style of triple beloved of the Italians, but contrapuntal, with a hint of the English song-style in the melodic material. A ballett such as this bears little relation to the Italian *balletto* of Gastoldi.

It is in his madrigals in five and six parts, published in 1600, that we can best appreciate the brilliance and impulsive boldness of Weelkes the madrigalist. He is entirely conversant with the problems of handling big sonorities, and will revel in the richness of a six-part texture for long stretches of a madrigal (e.g. *Like two proud armies* opens with over twenty bars of six-part tutti). Some of the most graphic portrayals of words occur in these tuttis: multiple melismas and inter-twining thirds create the right sound for 'a thund'ring fight' in the madrigal just mentioned, and for the 'sulphureous fire' of the volcano Hecla in that remarkable geographical madrigal, *Thule, the period of cosmography*, Weelkes's tour-de-force (Example 62). The D minor of this passage is especially effective after the relentless F major tonality of the music up to this point. At the words 'these things seem wondrous' Weelkes displays a splendid command of harmonic progression through keys related to F, which consists in outline of E♭, B♭, D minor, A major, C minor, G, and C major, with strong falling fourths in the bass. The C minor chord does not sound as surprising as it looks, being less a chromatic movement than a colouring of the final cadence. For real chromaticism we should look to the oddly contorted motive

Example 61
Weelkes, 'On the plains, fairy trains'

with which Weelkes chooses to show 'how strangely Fogo burns' in part II of this vast madrigal.

In *Like two proud armies* the metaphors are military, and Weelkes exploits the unusual SSATBB scoring to produce divided-choir effects between SAB and STB, closely overlapping so as to conjure up a battlefield encounter. The five-part madrigal *Cold winter's ice is fled* presents him in more melancholy vein, enjoying the possibilities of more intimate voice-groupings than in the large six-part works. Several delightful instances of contrast between upper and lower voices occur, of which the most attractive is the opening, with its appropriate minor inflection (Example 63). From the emotional point of view, this constitutes restraint, even understatement; an altogether more striking example, in harmonic terms, is the celebrated beginning of part II of *O care, thou wilt despatch me*, one of the most often quoted

Example 62

Weelkes, 'Thule, the period of cosmography'

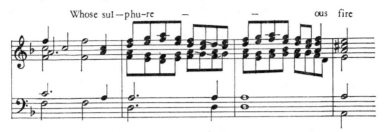

Example 63

Weelkes, 'Cold winter's ice is fled'

yet least representative passages in the whole English madrigal output. It is only here that an English madrigalist begins to approach the intensity of language typical of the Italian mannerists, and yet even the chromatic soprano line would hardly have shocked the admirers of Rore fifty years earlier. It is really in the novelty of modulation and key-sense that the significance of this passage lies; expressive as it may be, it seems too controlled and well-ordered to be strictly comparable to Wert or late Marenzio, whose approach might well have

been more devious. Quite possibly Italian precedents were far from
Weelkes's mind when he wrote it. That he should have done so is
consistent with his position as the boldest member of the English
school.

By comparison, a sense of restraint marks the work of the other
distinguished English madrigalist, John Wilbye (1574–1638). Like

Example 64 (a) and (b)
Wilbye, 'As matchless beauty'

Morley, he is happy to range over any texture from three to six voices
with equal assurance. His output is contained in two collections dated
1598 and 1609 respectively. The English penchant for musical organization in the madrigal is reflected in Wilbye's strong sense of formal
design. For instance, the four-part *As matchless beauty* is laid out in
AABCC form, with both first and last lines repeated; this is a typical
canzonet arrangement, yet this text is no canzonet poem, with its
obviously madrigalian contrasts. Wilbye's subtle contrapuntal touch
is apparent throughout: notice how he rearranges the fairly conventional strands of Example 64a when, a few bars later, he adds a
fourth voice (Example 64b). In general Wilbye is more interested in
spinning out a polyphonic fabric of infinite variety than in exploiting

harmony and sonority in the way that Weelkes does; with six voices, he prefers contrasted groupings to long, brilliant tuttis.

An unusually rich texture occurs in the five-part *Weep, weep, mine eyes*, a work whose uppermost voice has a song-like quality often found in Wilbye. It sounds like a monody scored for five voices, an impression confirmed by the declamatory chordal setting of the words

Example 65
Wilbye, 'Weep, weep, mine eyes'

'ay me, ah cruel fortune' after the double bar—the nearest any English composer came to Wert's technique of choral recitation. Wilbye's characteristic use of sequence—another structural means of articulating his music—is beautifully exemplified near the end (Example 65) as is also his free use of minor and major forms of the scale to point the mood of the text. Example 65, with its minor inflections and double suspensions, enhances the yearning feeling of the final couplet:

> I hope when I am dead in Elysian plain
> To meet, and there with joy we'll love again.

This use of major and minor becomes a structural device in the fine six-part *Draw on sweet night*. These opening words, set to gentle polyphony in D major, return with heightened emotional meaning after a troubled episode in a clear D minor ('my life so ill through want of comfort fares'); later the tonal sequence is reversed so that the madrigal ends in the minor after an episode in the major. Once again,

Example 66
Wilbye, 'Flora gave me fairest flowers'

this feel for distinctions of tonality can be seen to be symptomatic of the English desire for balanced formal schemes. The text of *Draw on sweet night* has a moral tone that places it closer to the English song tradition, a trait generally noticeable in Wilbye's second set of madrigals. Counterpoint that is abstract, though never dry or academic, serves ideally for such texts; Wilbye seems to abhor the chordal frivolities of the ballett. This loftiness of conception inspires his settings of canzonet texts, too. *Flora gave me fairest flowers* represents an example of a piece of comparative doggerel adorned with exquisite music in five parts. The setting of lines 3 and 4 is cleverly dovetailed, and Wilbye spends a long time lavishing playful music on the final couplet (lines 5 and 6). Example 66 shows the graceful treatment of the simple repetitive tonic-dominant progression, the second setting of the words 'come ye wantons'. Where the Italians might have confined the interplay to the two upper voices, Wilbye extends it to all the four above the bass.

The three madrigalists Morley, Weelkes and Wilbye are the most influential and versatile in a development that encompasses many minor figures, whose madrigals continued to appear after this triumvirate had finished with the genre in about 1610. The English madrigal melted away as quickly as it had appeared, for it lacked the essential nourishment from Italian sources and faced the competition of a new native genre, the lute-song. Morley himself, the high priest of the cult for things Italian, had died, probably in 1602, and the new style of Monteverdi's continuo madrigals, with its heightened technical demands and emphasis on drama, was not something that would interest the English. They had wanted a lightweight, polished music, not too serious and not too banal, and this they had found in the early Italian anthologies and in the work of the English madrigal school for whom the anthologies had been the starting point. It was not so much a case of manufacturing Italian music under licence, more one of transplanting carefully selected Italian roots on to English soil.

1. An extract of this translation is reprinted in Strunk, op. cit., p. 281 ff.
2. Quoted in M. C. Boyd, *Elizabethan Music and Musical Criticism*, 2nd ed. (Philadelphia, 1962), p. 208.
3. W. L. Woodfill, *Musicians in English Society* (Princeton, 1953), chap. ix.
4. op. cit., ch. iv.
5. ibid., pp. 123-4.
6. *The Musical Times*, cviii (1967), p. 736.
7. See Kerman's detailed analysis, op. cit., pp. 205 ff.

9

THE ITALIAN MADRIGAL AFTER 1600—

DECLINE OR TRANSFORMATION?

On the title page of Monteverdi's fifth book of madrigals we read that the collection has been issued

col basso continuo per il Clavicembano, Chitarrone, od altro simile istrumento; fatto particolarmente per li sei ultimi et per li altri a beneplacito

(with thorough-bass for harpsichord, chitarrone or similar instruments; particularly for the last six pieces and optional in the others)

The idea of the unaccompanied madrigal was already becoming an archaism, just as the idea of church music without a supporting organ did at the same time. But the introduction of the *basso continuo* was not then seen as a revolutionary event: in church music, certainly, the organ and other instruments had long been used to double or replace voices—the latter especially in places where choirs were inadequate to cope with involved polyphony—and a continuo organ part consisting of the bass line and a few indications of harmony was seen as a convenient way of notating what was becoming common practice. To a brilliant composer in the secular field like Monteverdi the continuo was more than a useful notational device: it opened up new possibilities of texture and scoring, and of musical construction on a large scale, and the picture of his later madrigals is one of a gradual but fascinating experimentation with these.

The last six madrigals in his Book V are not positively the first with continuo or accompaniment (there is always the danger in musical history that a first famous example will be assumed to be the first actual example of some development), a description which properly appertains to Luzzaschi's *Madrigali per cantare et sonare*, published in Rome in 1601.[1] These are historically important transitional pieces for one to three voices and fully written-out accompaniment, composed with brilliantly ornamental voice parts for the three ladies of Ferrara. If the medium is unique for this date in its anticipation of the Baroque cantata, at the same time the stylistic concept is of the late sixteenth century. It is simply as if one had taken a conventional madrigal scoring, applied authentic but extravagant ornamentation to the upper parts, and made the keyboard supply the remainder of the texture. In other words, these works are at once a written-out form of practices quite common in this virtuoso phase of the madrigal and an indication of how the advent of monody and the continuo would change its musical development.

Nevertheless, Luzzaschi's accompanied madrigals remained an isolated phenomenon; those in Monteverdi's Book V showed the way things were going, even if they appeared somewhat cautious. This, Monteverdi's last Mantuan collection, achieved considerable popularity through its several reprints in the ensuing years, perhaps precisely because it included a *basso continuo* part. To see what he could do with the new medium, however, we would do better to look to the next volume, published one year after he had gone to Venice as *maestro di cappella* at St Mark's in 1613. The sixth book, like its predecessor, contains a mixture of *concertato* works to which the continuo is indispensable, and others where it is inessential. Among the latter group are two of his most famous madrigal cycles, the tripartite *Lamento d'Arianna*, a rearrangement of part of the opera *Arianna* (1608), and the *Sestina*, in both of which he reconciles intense feeling and the unaccompanied polyphonic medium with great skill. If we compare these with the *concertato* pieces we can see how the typical 'trio' texture of the Baroque blossoms forth. In the unaccompanied madrigals trio groupings are frequently heard, but here all the parts are sung; where there is a continuo it supplies the lowest part of the trio, and all that is needed are two often equal upper parts (sopranos or tenors) to interweave or sing mellifluous thirds above it. If the bass voice is part of a trio, it simply follows the continuo. In order to satisfy his love for the duet-plus-bass sound, Monteverdi further transforms the conventional five-part texture SSATB into SSTTB, giving two pairs of equal voices, in *Qui rise Tirsi*. This is a work which also shows the spaciousness of musical design possible in the *concertato* style, because the inherent contrasts of utterance in this more ornamental manner of declamation allow of longer sections for the various voice groupings without amorphousness. And to give an overall shape to the work and provide points of reference among these long interludes, what better than a tutti refrain at the words 'O memoria felice'?

With this exciting concept of the alternation of solo and tutti and the lengthening of sections for different textures within a piece it is no

Example 67 (a) and (b)
Monteverdi, 'Presso un fiume tranquillo'
[For a thousand pains, let there be a thousand kisses]

surprise that Monteverdi should resume the development of the dialogue madrigal in the new context, and indeed Book VI concludes with a fine seven-part one, *Presso un fiume tranquillo*. The two lovers are represented by soprano and tenor, the other voices form a chorus which narrates, and all take up a gorgeous refrain at the end. At first the lovers each sing expressive solos, one of which (p. 118) trips along in a dainty *canzonetta* rhythm, but soon their dialogue overlaps until these magical sixths of the refrain (Example 67a). This is especially effective after the warlike metaphors and brilliant runs just before. In Example 67b we see how it is later taken over by the tutti, the bold contrary motion enriched by warm harmonies. Already present in the work is a hint of the secular cantata of the later Baroque.

As if to emphasize the uncertainty as to whether pieces like this really belonged to the madrigal genre at all, Monteverdi entitled the contents of his seventh book of madrigals *Concerto*—a suitably all-embracing and up-to-date designation for the immense variety of textures and techniques represented, from monodies to six-part pieces, with and without *obbligati* instruments. Published in 1619 as the fruits of Monteverdi's first few years at Venice, the collection stands as the secular parallel of developments that were also taking place in church music, and it might even be fair to say that, far from bringing him into contact only with conservative sacred music, his new church post might have resulted in some cross-fertilization between *concertato* sacred and secular styles. To say this is not, however, to diminish the importance of the monodists, and in particular the writers of pretty arias that were beginning to tickle the music-loving public's fancy at this time, even though Monteverdi never became a true monodist but always preferred the contrapuntal interplay possible with two or more voices and continuo.

Predictably enough it is the chamber duet for two voices and continuo that appears most frequently in Book VII—there are fourteen in all—as a result of Monteverdi's evident fascination with this texture in earlier works and also, no doubt, because this medium had proved extremely popular in the sacred context during the second decade of the century, particularly the context of evening devotion in princely apartments, where at other times secular pieces might be similarly performed. It is important to stress this inter-dependence of sacred and secular music not only because changes in musical taste affected both in the same way but also as a corrective to the oft-repeated view that advance could only occur in worldly music and never in sacred during the early Baroque. Thus, it is no more than coincidental to each's environment that Monteverdi's best duets are mainly secular, Grandi's and Donati's sacred. The declamatory and emotional musical language they speak is much the same.

Equally as important as the chamber duet was the trio, especially where the extra voice is a bass which doubles the continuo in outline, for while the contrapuntal possibilities are increased the scoring retains its duet-plus-bass composition. *Parlo miser o taccio* is a brilliant example of Monteverdi's approach to this challenge. It thrives not on luscious melodic beauty but on virtuosity of vocal technique—dotted rhythms and semiquavers—and of interplay, as is apparent at the very outset (Example 68). The ornamental nature of the vocal writing can be seen by comparing the bass voice-part to the continuo: Monteverdi

Example 68
Monteverdi, 'Parlo miser o taccio'
[I speak of misery, or not at all]

liked to write out such ormanents, where others might leave the singer to improvise them from a basic outline like this continuo part. The bass singer must have had a prodigious range, for this madrigal requires from him a high E and a low D, more than two octaves apart and joined by a continuous scale, at the end. Harmonically Monteverdi had left far behind the mere dominant sevenths that annoyed Artusi and was now refusing to resolve a grindingly dissonant ninth, all the more remarkable when it was in the bass—a striking representation of 'hardness of heart' (Example 69).

The only true monodies in Book VII are the two rather dry *lettere amorose*, the more appealing *Tempro la cetra* (pleasantly varied by an instrumental *ritornello*) and the remarkable *Con che soavità*, lavishly accompanied by three groups of plucked and bowed stringed instruments. Paradoxically enough, this is an amorous dialogue, in which the emotional rise and fall is coloured by the ever-changing scoring of the accompaniment. It is interesting that both this and *Presso un*

Example 69
Monteverdi, 'Parlo miser o taccio'
[To the hard heart]

fiume from Book VI end with the minor plagal cadence (G minor–D major): the final word is 'kisses', and there is no doubt that in this context the minor chord adds to the amorous atmosphere.

More important as a group are the two *canzonette* and one *romanesca*. The latter (*Ohimè, dov'è il mio ben?*) is a duet in four stanzas, each built upon the same ground bass, a stock formula for much light music of the time, while the former include the famous *Chiome d'oro*, with its delightful *ritornello* for two violins cleverly divided up over a thrice-repeated *ostinato* bass and interspersed between each line of vocal duet, and *Amor che deggio far*, similarly laid out but with four voices and the more four-square rhythms of Vecchi's *canzonette*. Their importance lies in the use of *ostinato* bass patterns to add coherence with the mixed medium of voices, violins and continuo. The idea of a violin refrain was not itself a novelty: Monteverdi had tried it out in the *Scherzi Musicali* of 1607.

It was nineteen years before Monteverdi published his Book VIII, enigmatically entitled *Madrigali guerrieri ed amorosi* (1638). In the preface he explained the meaning of the 'warlike genus' represented in certain of the new madrigals, in which very rapid repeated notes (*stile concitato*) conveyed the passion, anger and other violent emotions that were as much part of human make-up as those others more usually encountered in madrigalian psychology. Though on the face of it this idea—particularly its musical realization—may have seemed revolutionary (indeed it was one of Monteverdi's few actually epoch-making innovations), there had been precedents for a graphic representation in music of warlike sounds such as Jannequin's chanson *La guerre* and a Venetian 'battle' canzona by Andrea Gabrieli based on Jannequin, and certain military metaphors had long been part and parcel of madrigalian poetic imagery.

Book VIII is clearly divided into two parts, the 'warlike' and 'amorous' pieces, the former containing a dramatic *scena* (*Il combattimento di Tancredi e Clorinda*) which, though not belonging to the history of the madrigal, in 1624 first displayed Monteverdi's new *stile concitato*. For the rest, the whole collection is a contrast between intimate chamber music that follows naturally on from the smaller-scale music in Book VII and large-scale works with many voices and instruments. The first one of these in the 'warlike' part of Book VIII (*Altri canti d'amor*) shows how, despite the size of the canvas on which Monteverdi was painting and the varied colours he had at his disposal, he failed to achieve a satisfying overall structure even though the final choral section is a varied repeat of the previous bass solo. The warlike section, too, with its repeated notes, fanfares and rushing scales, sticks out a little self-consciously from the whole. More convincing is the wonderful *Hor ch'el ciel e la terra*, which could almost be called a tone-poem, with its opening mood of quiet and peace at night captured by the lowest registers of all the voices in much the same way as he painted the words 'et in terra pax' in his *Gloria à 7*. The passionate feelings of unrequited love suddenly manifest themselves and are worked up by a tenor duet, pitted against brusque interjections by the tutti and several utterances of the word 'piango' to a quite old-fashioned dissonant formula, and the *prima parte* concludes with several pages of warlike raging, realizing the lover's interior torment. The vivid contrast between this passage and the beginning of the piece, and the way in which the initial mood is engulfed by a torrent of passion, are both thoroughly Baroque, as is the addition of idiomatic violin parts to the six-part vocal ensemble.

To Einstein, one of the last historians to speak of the early Baroque in terms of the decline, or even the death, of the madrigal, this music stood worlds apart from the true spirit of the genre, which had been dispelled with the arrival of the continuo and the emancipation of instrumental accompaniment. More recent commentators have inclined to a liberal interpretation of the word madrigal, whose essence simply implies a non-strophic composition based on a serious poetic text treated with expressive respect, so that the creations of Monteverdi's later years have come to be viewed as madrigals (which is what after all, he called them) transformed into the expressive and colouristic context of their period. Indeed, one may ask with Denis Stevens when (after 1619 and Monteverdi's Book VII) is a madrigal not a concerto?[2] and not when is a madrigal not a madrigal? One thing of which we should beware is dubbing these late works cantatas merely on the grounds of their sectional construction, for this is to cut them off from the madrigal tradition. They should be seen in the broadest possible light, in such a way that confusing historical demarcations are avoided. In truth, if the madrigal became less and less fashionable in the seventeenth century, this was because of the changing musical exigencies of the period, especially the rise of opera as court and public entertainment, and of instrumental music for amateur music-making, not because the spirit of the madrigal had been sacrificed on the altar of Baroque innovations viewed in abstract.

In any case, it is perhaps misleading to speak of a decline in madrigal-singing until much later in the seventeenth century than has popularly been supposed, as Gloria Rose has pointed out.[3] She found evidence of some 450 surviving madrigal publications after 1600, which flies in the face of regretful remarks, usually by composers prefacing their own music and hoping for a sale, about the scarcity of madrigals and the paucity of performances. For instance, here is Domenico Mazzocchi (to whose music we shall return) writing a preface in 1638 at Rome:

The most artistic study known to music is that of the madrigal; but few are being composed today and even fewer sung, they being to their misfortune all but banished from the academies.[4]

T.M.—F*

The publication itself—*Madrigali a cinque voci ed altri varii concerti*—is by no means the 'last fling' in a dying form of music that we might expect it to be from such a plaint: it is typical of many early Baroque madrigal collections in dividing the contents into *concertato* (with continuo), and unaccompanied together with a third group labelled 'variamente concertati'. Ever since Monteverdi's Book V younger composers had been bringing mixed collections like this into print, and the madrigal-buying public, far from being out of their depth with the new style, apparently preferred accompanied pieces; for they were quick to avail themselves of formerly *a cappella* collections reissued with added continuo. So did the composers, who praised the 'better results' achieved by the use of accompaniment. This itself led of course to new textures with two, three or four voices as well as the established five- and six-part ones: Monteverdi's Book VII was no isolated phenomenon and should be seen as following current taste rather than dictating it.

Mazzocchi's madrigals of 1638, in keeping to the five-part scoring, are perhaps retrospective, and the unaccompanied pieces in particular could have been written anything up to thirty years earlier by the young Monteverdi or Schütz; but we have come to expect conservatism from Romans (Marenzio was a notable exception), for they had not the stimulus of those progressive styles whose testing ground had always been northern Italy. The fact is that, scoring apart, these are as excitingly modern as any early Baroque madrigals and there is no evidence that Mazzocchi was trying hard to breathe a kiss of life into a moribund form, as we can see from a selection that was reprinted not long ago.[5] Of the unaccompanied madrigals, *Di marmo siete voi*, with its intense text by Marini, has an appropriately cold and marble-like opening of 6/3 chords and repeated notes, not unlike recitative translated into the context of part music, and recalling Monteverdi's madrigal adaptation of the monodic *Lamento d'Arianna*. Mazzocchi has a competent way with contrasted motives in counterpoint, or bringing voices in to make a pungent dissonance. It is worth quoting one couplet in full to show these traits and also the beautiful contrast of colours (Example 70). Particularly powerful is the use of the dominant seventh in unusual inversions, marked by asterisks, quite apart from the 9–8 suspension of the fifth bar, and the momentary diminished seventh with the first tenor's B♮ near the cadence. Slurred leading notes, another modern declamatory touch, abound too. *Fuggi, fuggi* is

Example 70
Mazzocchi, 'Di marmo siete voi'
[In loving and in being
 I am constant, you are hard]

also a fine piece, culminating in a superb tour-de-force of Baroque counterpoint as the steady rising crotchets of one idea march against a more agitated descending phrase. The remarkable final climax occurs under a ringing pedal note that gives rise to harmonies almost unthinkable in the seventeenth century (Example 71).

Example 71
Mazzocchi, 'Fuggi, fuggi'
[Of what use is flight?
 He has already been taken away to his death]

The *concertato* pieces in this collection are just as fascinating, if in different ways. In the very distinct alternation of complex rapid contrapuntal passage work and slower, more dissonant strains they recall Gesualdo, whom Mazzocchi praises in his preface. But the Roman has a much clearer feel for tonal direction and modulation, and his music does not meander. Towards the end of *Pian piano* there occurs a curious passage in F♯ major, but although the final G major cadence sounds apologetic, the harmonic progression that links the two keys has a forward momentum and contains no inconsequential juxtapositions in Gesualdo's manner.

So far only the polyphonic madrigals of the seventeenth century have been discussed and there has been little occasion to lend much importance to the growth of monody as a major factor in changes of style. Its importance is central to secular song and opera and tangential to the madrigal, where it shows its face in the more general use of declamatory expression, or in the occasional elaborate solos found in Monteverdi's last works in the form. But this should not blind us to the fact that, for those pioneers of the *nuove musiche* to whom setting an Italian text for more than one voice at a time was anathema (by destroying audibility and expressive potential), there was a short period in which the monodic material for solo voice and continuo flourished. Its exponents were members (e.g. Giulio Caccini) or followers (e.g. Sigismondo d'India) of the Florentine Camerata, who had felt that a polyphonic madrigal was a travesty of the text, a contradiction in terms. There was in fact nothing new about solo song, or even virtuoso solo-singing, which was becoming increasingly important in the polyphonic madrigal, and the desire of the Camerata was to some extent a negative one in that they intended at all costs to discredit polyphony. It was one of their members, Caccini, who codified new techniques of expressive singing and ornamentation, and it was in the field of the solo madrigal rather than operatic recitative that these ideas first flowered musically. Compared with such solo song, contained in Caccini's epoch-making *Le nuove musiche* of 1602, the earliest operas which for some reason so fascinated earlier historians seem esoteric and lacking in direction.

Our liberal definition of the term 'madrigal' must then include these monodic works, which deserve a wider familiarity than they have had in the past. While such virtuoso music fulfilled a different function from the polyphonic madrigal, being a preserve of the courts where talented soloists were available, it coexisted quite happily with it, and indeed d'India was able to turn his hand to either type. For even though the original Camerata had hoped to oust polyphony, they never succeeded and it would be futile to try and view the two styles as being in competition, especially when the polyphonic madrigal so readily adapted certain expressive techniques from monody.

One of Caccini's most famous solo madrigals was *Amarilli mia bella*, whose lyrical flow of melody is carefully laid out in an ABB form that lends musical shape. The B sections end with a finely-controlled build-up of feeling through the increasingly passionate incantations

Example 72
Caccini, 'Amarilli mia bella'
[Amarillis is my love]

of 'Amarilli', and Caccini provides a masterly stroke at the very end (Example 72), for whereas the B section first concluded with the G minor cadence in the seventh bar, he now adds an even more heightened cry to bring the music to a close in G major. Apart from occasional affective intervals like the diminished fourth near the opening, the harmonic style is placid and conventional; and musical interest has to be vested in the beauties of the melodic line and its ornamentation. The continuo is purely accompanimental and there is none of the interplay between bass line and voice found in early solo motets, which can sound a little like counterpoint *manqué*, even though Caccini occasionally allowed this elsewhere.

D'India was not such an avowed anti-contrapuntist, for he wrote polyphonic madrigals as well as solo ones. He was also more keen to introduce chromatic elements into his expressive vocabulary though these had proved distasteful to the followers of the Camerata, who had looked upon them as further examples of the iniquities of the polyphonic madrigal. A fine example of this is the rising chromatic melody over a descending bass at the beginning of *O dolcezze amarissime*

Example 73
d'India, 'O dolcezze amarissime'
[O, when (love) is lost every memory of it disappears]

(*Musiche*, 1609), which later shows some very subtle harmonic turns (Example 73). We can see here how d'India likes to contrive an affective augmented triad at cadence points, and how he manages to confound aural expectations at two asterisked points: the E♮ he twists from a

Example 74
d'India, 'Cruda Amarilli'
[Cruel Amarillis, whose name is still sweet, alas . . .]

chromatic passing note to the dominant of A minor, while the C sounds oddly non-functional between the two flanking harmonies. The setting of Guarini's *Cruda Amarilli* opens with a melodic sentence whose beauty lies not only in the crowning ornament on 'lasso' but also in the appoggiaturas of the first two phrases and the repetition of 'd'amar' (Example 74). D'India is well able to avoid the monotony of too many perfect cadences which plagues the work of lesser men, by making his cadences actually join poetic lines rather than mark them off in non-continuous sections.

But despite this progressive wave of solo-madrigal composition by d'India and his contemporaries, this monodic genre had but a short life, as popular fancy was turning more and more to the tuneful aria, and the publications were reflecting the change of taste. Apart from the question of fashion, we can see the same musical developments at work as affected the polyphonic madrigal. The *concertato* style, with the new palette of colours it offered the composer, demanded new musical solutions to problems of structural clarity and contrast—solutions that were attempted by Monteverdi and others in the polyphonic field. In that of monody a musical organization not present in the wayward strains of chromatic madrigals was just as necessary, and the development of the strophic aria with the possibilities of variation over an *ostinato* bass of clear harmonic patterns provided a satisfying answer. The year 1620 marked the beginning of the heyday of the solo aria, and it is not without significance that other indications of preference for a more tautly organized musical structure—e.g. Monteverdi's *canzonette* of Book VII or the rondo-form approach for psalm-settings in church music—date from this time.

The development of the madrigal, then, ends with an apparent paradox. Monody comes, not to sweep the madrigal away, but to enhance its tendencies towards Baroque expressionism. The monodic madrigal dies out, unable to be adapted to changing taste, while the polyphonic variety has a new lease of life, albeit in transformed guise, to peter out only gradually in the middle of the century, for even the Baroque era does not see an end to the wish of cultured people to sit round a table and sing.

1. Reprinted in *Monumenti di Musica Italiana*, Series ii, ii (Brescia, 1965).

2. *The Monteverdi Companion* (London, 1968), p. 228.

3. 'Polyphonic Italian Madrigals of the seventeenth century', *Music & Letters*, xlvii (1966), p. 153.

4. Quoted in Einstein, op. cit., ii, p. 868.

5. *Das Chorwerk*, xcv (Wolfenbüttel, 1965).

SOURCE-LIST OF MADRIGALS

This is a complete alphabetical list of all madrigals discussed in the foregoing text
Explanations of abbreviations will be found on page 159.

Title	Composer	Source
Ah, dolente partita	Wert	GA p. 71
Al merto et al valore	Hassler	DTB xx, 137
Al vag'e incerto gioco di primiera	Striggio	EIM iii, 285
Alla dolce ombra	Rore	CE iv, 7
Alla riva del Tebro	Palestrina	CE xxxi, 47
		HAM i, 155
Alma cortese e bella	G. Gabrieli	AMI ii, 155
Alma nemes	Lassus	CE (old) iii, 169
Altri canti d'amor	Monteverdi	CE viii, 2
Amarilli mia bella	Caccini	GMB p. 193
Amfiparnaso, L'	Vecchi	CP v
Amor, ben mi credevo	Rore	CE iv, 28
		CW v, 21
Amor che deggio far	Monteverdi	CE vii, 182
Amor mi fa morire	Willaert	EIM iii, 59
April is in my mistress' face	Morley	EM ii, 1
Ardo, si	Hassler	DTB xx, 6
As matchless beauty	Wilbye	EM vii, 77
Aspro cor	Parabosco	CW cv, 14
	Wert	CE i, 33
Calami sonum ferentes	Rore	Burney H iii, 319
Cantai, or piango	Lassus	CE (old) ii, 1
	Wert	CE ii, 32
Carlo ch'en tenerella acerba etade	Monte	DTÖ lxxvii, 1
Ch'ami la vita mia	Bertani	KSS No. 705, p. 81
Che fai alma	Donato	CW cv, 35

Title	Composer	Source
Chi la gagliarda	Donato	AMI i, 183
	Nola	EIM iii, 80
Chi vuol'udir'	Marenzio	Arnold M p. 5
Chiare, fresch'e dolci acque	Arcadelt	EIM iii, 125
		CE vii, 162
	Palestrina	CE ii, 107
Chichilichi	Nola	EIM iii, 83
Chiome d'oro	Monteverdi	CE vii, 176
Cold winter's ice is fled	Weelkes	EM xi, 1
Come fuggir	Marenzio	KSS No. 705, p. 48
Come la notte	Lassus	CE (new) i, 136
Come lieta si mostra	C. Festa	RE p. 197
Come woeful Orpheus	Byrd	EM xvi, 98
Con che soavità	Monteverdi	CE vii, 137
Cruda Amarilli	d'India	IM ser. I, iv, 82
	Monteverdi	CE v, 1
Crudele acerba	Lassus	CE (old) ii, 44
	Marenzio	Arnold M p. 72
	Wert	CE ix, 38
		EIM iii, 208
Cruel, wilt thou persever?	Morley	EM iii, 55
Da le belle contrade	Rore	CW v, 24
		HAM i, 142
Deep lamenting	Morley	EM i, 44
Deh come trista dei	Arcadelt	CE vi, 15
Del crud'amor	Ferretti	EIM iii, 234
Di marmo siete voi	Mazzocchi	CW xcv, 20
Die now, my heart	Morley	EM ii, 92
Discolorato hai, morte	Taglia	CW lxxxviii, 21
Dolcissima mia vita	Gesualdo	CE v, 23
		GMB p. 178
Dolorosi martir	Marenzio	Einstein M i, 16
(in English)		Ed. Harman (S & B)
Donna ne fu	C. Festa	Wagner MP p. 487
Dormend'un giorno a Bai	Verdelot	Wagner MP p. 461
Draw on sweet night	Wilbye	EM vii, 201
Dunque addio	Schütz	CE xxii, 103
Dur'è'l partito	C. Festa	EIM iii, 33
Ecco ch'un altra volta	Wert	CE ix, 5
		CW cix, 6
Ecco l'aurora	A. Gabrieli	GA p. 32
Erasi al sole	Porta	GA p. 59
Felici d'Adria	A. Gabrieli	Arnold G p. 64
Festino nella sera del giovedì grasso	Banchieri	CP i
Fiere silvestre	Marenzio	GA p. 65
Flora gave me fairest flowers	Wilbye	EM vi, 103

Title	Composer	Source
Fuggi, fuggi	Mazzocchi	CW xcv, 25
Fuggi o mio core	Schütz	CE xxii, 51
Fummo felici	Vecchi	GA p. 76
		CP viii, 40
Già fu chi m'hebbe cara	Monte	DTÖ lxxvii, 67
Gite, rime dolenti	Arcadelt	CE vii, 86
		CW lviii, 1
Giunto alla tomba	Wert	CE vii, 38
		EIM iii, 221
Hard by a crystal fountain	Morley	EM xxxii, 238
Hor ch'el ciel e la terra	Monteverdi	CE viii, 39
I vidi in terra	Donato	CW cv, 23
I'vo piangendo	A. Gabrieli	Arnold G p. 52
	Zarlino	CW lxxvii, 24
Il bianco e dolce cigno	Arcadelt	CE ii, 38
Il cicalamento delle donne al bucato	Striggio	CP iv
Il combattimento di Tancredi e Clorinda	Monteverdi	CE viii, 132
Ingiustissimo amor	della Viola	CW lviii, 18
Ingredere	Corteccia	RE p. 104
Io son amore	Marenzio	Arnold M p. 2
Io son ferito	Hassler	DTB ix, 24
Itene mie querele	Luzzaschi	EIM iii, 262
Itene o miei sospiri	Gesualdo	CE v, 19
Lagrime di San Pietro	Lassus	CW xxxiv, xxxvii, xli
L'amanza mia	Azzaiolo	
Lamento d'Arianna	Monteverdi	CE vi, 1
Lasso, perché mi fuggi	Grabbe	CW xxxv, 4
Laura soave	A. Gabrieli	Ed. Arnold (Schott)
Leggiadretto Clorino	Vecchi	KSS No. 705, p. 68
Like two proud armies	Weelkes	EM xii, 1
Luci serene e chiare	Gesualdo	CE iv, 13
L'ultimo dì di maggio	S. Festa	
Madonna il tuo bel viso	Verdelot	EIM iii, 29
Madonna io vi confesso	Gero	Wagner MP p. 483
Madonna mia gentil	Marenzio	HAM i, 177
Madonna non so dir	Verdelot	CW v, 13
Madonna qual certezza	Verdelot	EIM iii, 21
Madonna quand'io penso	Nasco	CW lviii, 25
Madonn'io non lo so	Nola	CW viii, 13
	Willaert	CW viii, 18
Matona mia cara	Lassus	CE (old) x, 93
Mentre ch'el cor	Willaert	CE xiii, 32
		CW v, 5
Mentre il cuculo	Caimo	EIM iii, 237
Mentre l'un polo	Striggio	CW lxxx, 27

Title	Composer	Source
Mentre nel dubbio petto	C. Festa	CW lviii, 13
Misera, non credea	Wert	CE viii, 29
		CW lxxx, 10
Moro lasso al mio duolo	Gesualdo	CE vi, 74
Non è lasso martire	Rore	CW v, 28
Non vedi o sacr'Apollo	A. Gabrieli	Arnold G p. 31
Now is the month of Maying	Morley	EM iv, 8
O bella, o bianca più	Vecchi	KSS No. 705, p. 62
O bene mio	Willaert	CW v, 12
O care thou wilt despatch me	Weelkes	EM xi, 19
O com'è gran martire	Monteverdi	CE iii, 8
O dolcezze amarissime	d'India	IM ser. I, iv, 119
O felici occhi miei	Arcadelt	CE ii, 82
		CW v, 19
O fere stelle	Marenzio	EIM iii, 252
O messaggi del cor	Vicentino	CE p. 106
O morte, eterno fin	Rore	GA p. 13
O occhi manza mia	Lassus	CE (old) x, 103
O passi sparsi	S. Festa	Haar CM p. 229
O voi che sospirate	Marenzio	Einstein M i, 69
Occhi piangete	Lassus	CE (old) viii, 19
		CW xiii, 4
Ogn'hor per voi sospiro	Verdelot	EIM iii, 24
Ohimè, dov'è il mio ben?	Monteverdi	CE vii, 152
On a fair morning	Morley	EM ii, 109
On the plains, fairy trains	Weelkes	EM x, 17
Ove tra l'herbe e i fiori	Croce	Kerman EM p. 286
Oyme oyme	Cambio	CW viii, 20
	Nola	CW viii, 11
Parlo miser o taccio	Monteverdi	CE vii, 116
Pian piano	Mazzocchi	CW xcv, 9
Più che mai vaga	C. Festa	RE p. 171
Presso un fiume tranquillo	Monteverdi	CE vi, 113
Prophetiae Sybillarum	Lassus	CW xlviii
Qual mormorio soave	Marenzio	Arnold M p. 54
Quand'io ero giovinetto	G. Gabrieli	GA p. 44
Quand'io penso al martire	Merulo	GA p. 21
Quando la sera	Azzaiolo	
Quando nascesti, amor	Willaert	CE xiii, 103
Quando ritrova	C. Festa	HAM i, 140
Quant'ahi lasso	Verdelot	Wagner MP p. 464
Quant'è Madonna mia	C. Festa	Mald P xxvi, 19
Qui rise Tirsi	Monteverdi	CE vi, 77
Quivi sospiri	Luzzaschi	GA p. 53
Ride la primavera	Schütz	CE xxii, 43

Title	Composer	Source
Ridon di maggio	Hassler	DTB ix, 5
Sacri di Giove	G. Gabrieli	AMI ii, 159
Sacro tempio d'honor	G. Gabrieli	AMI ii, 149
Scendi dal paradiso	Marenzio	Einstein M ii, 12
Se ben il duol	Rore	CE iv, 107
Se la mia vita	Marenzio	Arnold M p. 32
Se per honesti preghi	Corteccia	AMI i, 113
Sestina	Monteverdi	CE vi, 46
Sfogava con le stelle	Monteverdi	CE iv, 15
Shoot false love I care not	Morley	EM iv, 4
Si ch'io vorrei morire	Monteverdi	CE iv, 78
Signor le tue man sante	G. Gabrieli	Ed. Kenton
		(Chappell)
S'infinita bellezza	Arcadelt	CE vii, 120
		GA p. 7
Sing we at pleasure	Weelkes	EM x, 51
Solo e pensoso	Marenzio	GMB p. 174
	Wert	CE vii, 32
		CW lxxx, 1
Spesso in poveri alberghi	Lassus	CE (old) viii, 83
		CW xiii, 7
Tanto mi trovo	Anon.	Haar CM p. 235
Tempro la cetra	Monteverdi	CE vii, 2
This sweet and merry month of May	Byrd	EM xvi, 42
Though Amaryllis dance	Byrd	EM xiv, 60
Thule, the period of cosmography	Weelkes	EM xii, 44
Tirsi morir volea	Marenzio	Einstein M i, 12
(in English)		Ed. Harman
		(S & B)
To shorten winter's sadness	Weelkes	EM x, 5
Tre ciechi siamo	Nola	CW xliii, 13
Tutte le vecchie	Maio	EIM iii, 79
Usciva omai	Wert	CE viii, 19
		CW cix, 12
Vaghi boschetti	Wert	CE vii, 22
		CW cix, 1
Valle che de'lamenti	Taglia	CW lxxxviii, 29
Verament'in amore	Monte	GA p. 40
Vergine il cui figliol	G. Gabrieli	Ed. Kenton
		(Chappell)
Vergine pura	Monte	CE vi, 13
Viva sempre in ogn'estate	Donato	AMI i, 175
Viver lieto voglio	Gastoldi	Gastoldi B p. 9
Voi mi poneste in foco	Arcadelt	CE vii, 183
		GMB p. 96
	Palestrina	CE ii, 127

Source-list of madrigals

Title	Composer	Source
Voi ve n'andate	Arcadelt	CE ii, 130
		CW v, 16
		HAM i, 141
Weep, weep, mine eyes	Wilbye	EM vii, 138
What is our life?	Gibbons	EM v, 88
Zoia zentil	Willaert	CW viii, 8

Collected editions (CE)

Arcadelt	*Opera Omnia*, Ed. A. Seay (Corpus Mensurabilis Musicae 31), 1965–
Gesualdo	*Sämtliche Madrigale*, Ed. W. Weissmann, 1957–62
Lassus	(old) *Sämtliche Werke*, Ed. F. Haberl and A. Sandberger, 1894–1953
	(new) *Sämtliche Werke* (Neue Reihe), Ed. W. Boetticher *et. al.* 1956–
Monte	*Opera*, Ed. C. van den Borren *et al.*, 1927–39
Monteverdi	*Tutte le Opere*, Ed. G. F. Malipiero, 1926–42
Palestrina	*Opere Complete*, Ed. R. Casimiri *et. al.*, 1939–
Rore	*Opera Omnia*, Ed. B. Meier (Corpus Mensurabilis Musicae 14), 1959–
Schütz	*Sämtliche Werke* (Neue Reihe), various editors, 1955–
Vicentino	*Opera Omnia*, Ed. H. Kaufmann (Corpus Mensurabilis Musicae 26), 1963
Wert	*Opera Omnia*, Ed. C. MacClintock (Corpus Mensurabilis Musicae 24), 1961–
Willaert	*Opera Omnia*, Ed. H. Zenck and W. Gerstenberg (Corpus Mensurabilis Musicae 3), 1950–

Other sources and explanation of abbreviations

AMI	L. Torchi, *L'Arte Musicale in Italia*, 1897
Arnold G	A. Gabrieli, *Ten Madrigals*, Ed. D. Arnold, 1970
Arnold M	L. Marenzio, *Ten Madrigals*, Ed. D. Arnold, 1966
Burney H	C. Burney, *A General History of Music*, 1776–89
CE	Collected editions (see page 159)
CP	*Capolavori Polifonici del Secolo XVI*, Ed. B. Somma, A. Schinetti, W. Martin, 1939–
CW	*Das Chorwerk*, various editors, 1929–
DTB	*Denkmäler der Tonkunst in Bayern*, 1900–31
DTÖ	*Denkmäler der Tonkunst in Österreich*, 1894–
EIM	A. Einstein, *The Italian Madrigal*, 1949
Einstein M	L. Marenzio, *Sämtliche Madrigale*, Ed. A. Einstein, 1929–31
EM	*The English Madrigalists*, Ed. E. Fellows, 1914–24
GA	*The Golden Age of the Madrigal*, Ed. A. Einstein, 1942
Gastoldi B	G. Gastoldi, *Balletti*, Ed. M. Sanvoisin (Le Pupitre 10), 1968
GMB	A. Schering, *Geschichte der Musik in Beispielen*, 1931

Haar CM   J. Haar (Ed.), *Chanson and Madrigal 1480–1530*, 1964
HAM   A. Davison and W. Apel, *Historical Anthology of Music*, 1946
IM   *Instituta et Monumenta*, Ed. F. Mompellio, 1970
Kerman EM   J. Kerman, *The Elizabethan Madrigal*, 1962
KSS   *Kalmus Study Score*, 1968
Mald P   R. Maldeghem, *Trésor Musical, Musique profane*, 1865–93
RE   *A Renaissance Entertainment*, Ed. A. C. Minor and B. Mitchell, 1968
S & B   Stainer and Bell (offprint)
Wagner MP   P. Wagner, 'Das Madrigal und Palestrina' in *Vierteljahrschrift für Musikwissenschaft*, viii (1892), p. 423

BIBLIOGRAPHY

The following books and articles are recommended for further information on:

1. *The madrigal in general*

E. Dent, 'The musical form of the madrigal', *Music & Letters* xi (1930)
A. Einstein, *The Italian Madrigal* (Princeton, 1949)
A. Einstein, 'Narrative rhythm in the madrigal', *Musical Quarterly*, xxix (1943)
G. Reese, *Music in the Renaissance* (London, 1954)

2. *The beginnings of the madrigal*

J. Haar (Ed.), *Chanson and Madrigal 1480-1530* (Cambridge, Mass., 1964)
E. Helm, 'Heralds of the Italian madrigal', *Musical Quarterly*, xxvii (1941)
D. Mace, 'Pietro Bembo and the literary origins of the Italian madrigal', *Musical Quarterly*, lv (1969)
D. Palmenac, 'The recently discovered complete copy of A. Antico's *Frottole intabulate* (1517)' in *Aspects of Medieval and Renaissance Music*, Ed. J. La Rue (New York, 1966)

3. *Madrigals by individual composers*

D. Arnold, *Marenzio* (London, 1965)
D. Arnold, *Monteverdi* (London, 1963)
D. Arnold, ' "Seconda prattica": a background to Monteverdi's madrigals', *Music & Letters*, xxxviii (1957)
D. Arnold, 'Thomas Weelkes and the madrigal', *Music & Letters* xxxi (1950)
D. Arnold and N. Fortune (Eds.), *The Monteverdi Companion* (London, 1968)
D. Brown, *Thomas Weelkes: a Biographical and Critical Study* (London, 1969)
N. Fortune, 'Sigismondo d'India—an introduction to his life and works', *Proceedings of the Royal Musical Association*, lxxxi (1954-5)
C. Gray and P. Heseltine, *Carlo Gesualdo* (London, 1926)

E. Kenton, *Life and Works of Giovanni Gabrieli* (Rome, 1967)
C. MacClintock, 'Some thoughts on the secular music of Giaches de Wert', *Musica Disciplina*, x (1956)
H. Moser, *Heinrich Schütz*, trans. C. Pfatteicher (St Louis, 1959)
J. Roche, *Palestrina* (London, 1971)
D. Stevens, *Thomas Tomkins 1572–1656* (New York, 1967)
J. E. Uhler, 'Thomas Morley's Madrigals for 4 voices', *Music & Letters*, xxxvi (1955)

4. *The madrigal in individual countries*

C. van den Borren, 'The æsthetic value of the English madrigal', *Proceedings of the Musical Association*, lii (1925–6)
E. Fellowes, *The English Madrigal* (London, 1925)
E. Fellowes, *The English Madrigal Composers*, 2nd ed. (London, 1948)
J. Kerman, *The Elizabethan Madrigal* (New York, 1962)
B. Pattison, *Music and Poetry in the English Renaissance* (London, 1948)
J. Trend, 'Spanish Madrigals', *Proceedings of the Musical Association*, lii (1925–6)
W. Woodfill, *Musicians in English Society* (Princeton, 1953)

5. *The seventeenth-century madrigal*

N. Fortune, 'Italian secular monody 1600–1635: an introductory survey', *Musical Quarterly*, xxxiv (1953)
G. Rose, 'Polyphonic Italian madrigals of the seventeenth century', *Music & Letters*, xlvii (1966)

6. *Madrigal texts*

A. Einstein, 'Italian madrigal verse', *Proceedings of the Musical Association*, lxiii (1936–7)

7. *Madrigals for special occasions*

A. C. Minor and B. Mitchell (Eds.), *A Renaissance Entertainment* (Missouri, 1968)
D. P. Walker, *Les Fêtes du Mariage . . .* (Paris, 1963)

8. *Musical æsthetics and the madrigal*

T. Morley, *A Plain & Easy Introduction to Practical Music*, Ed. R. A. Harman (London, 1952)
J. Shearman, *Mannerism* (London, 1967)
O. Strunk, *Source Readings in Music History* (New York, 1950)

INDEX